BILLIE JEAN

BILLIE JEAN

BY BILLIE JEAN KING

with Frank Deford

THE VIKING PRESS   NEW YORK

Grateful acknowledgment is made to Lenono Music for
permission to reprint a selection from "Watching the Wheels"
by John Lennon. Copyright © 1980 by
Lenono Music, BMI. All rights reserved.

Library of Congress Cataloging in Publication Data
King, Billie Jean.
Billie Jean.
1. King, Billie Jean.   2. Tennis players—United States—Biography.
I. Deford, Frank.   II. Title.
GV994.K56A35   796.342'092'4   [B]   81-71239
ISBN 0-670-47843-1   AACR2

Printed in the United States of America
Set in Linotron Aster

For LWK,
love forever

I have always disliked the labels that were arbitrarily placed on me, whether in feminist, heroic, or less flattering terms. This book may serve to remove some of those misconceptions. At times I may be tough and at other times extremely sensitive. I'm an individual. Those closest to me have always recognized this, and have allowed me to be my own person. To them, I offer thanks for their understanding, and for their advice and encouragement on this book. I would also like to thank all the thousands of people who took the time to write their words of support and encouragement.

CONTENTS

BILLIE
JEAN

1 GOING PUBLIC

On the night of May 5, 1981, a Tuesday, I was playing the first round in a tournament at a resort near Orlando, Florida. In fact, that night I was eliminated in the first round by Susie Rollinson, who had never been ranked better than one hundred and fifty in the world. The reason that I lost was that I didn't have much enthusiasm for playing, and even if I did, I just wasn't very good anymore. I didn't have any alibis. Susie Rollinson had lots of company those days. For the past couple years, I had made a lot of other unknowns happy and famous for a day, taking their place in the I-Beat-Billie-Jean Club. It's okay; you take scalps on the way up and lose your own on the way down. I was thirty-seven years old, zero-for-two in knees, and every year it was getting more difficult for me to breathe properly.

People hold a lot of misconceptions about me, and one of them, I know, is this: They're going to have to carry the old

1

lady out of the arena kicking and screaming. Boy, she is such a ham and needs that spotlight so much that she will never go softly into the night. In fact, though, like a lot of things people assume about me, that is not true. I do love tennis and I love the show, and if I'd only reached tenth, or maybe even third or fourth in the world, then I might very well have tried to hang on forever by my fingertips. When it's passed you by, it really doesn't make a great deal of difference whether you were three or thirty-three or a hundred and thirty-three. But if you've been number one, if you've been there, then it's a different trip altogether.

Once I realized that it was physically impossible for me to be the best anymore, then accepting the fact that I had to leave the courts was not hard. I probably would have even phased myself out long before Orlando, but in doubles, which I love, you can get by longer with your head instead of your legs. So I hung around for that, trying to figure out exactly how to make the complete break. I still had a few tournament commitments, and my husband, Larry, was starting up World Team Tennis again in the summer, so I had to stay in reasonable shape for that. Maybe I'd play doubles one more time at the French and at Wimbledon and at the U.S. Open. But whatever, it was just a peaceful winding down. In my own mind, I was finished as a professional tournament player.

But far from being down, I was on one of the great highs of my life. I was so happy I was even determined to lose a few pounds off of my fat little el chubbo legs. I still had a lot of endorsements, and the largest deal of my life was 90 percent finalized. There was going to be a "Wimbledon" tennis-clothing line, and I was to be the primary representative in the advertising and promotion. This was a marketing natural. I've won twenty Wimbledon championships, more than anybody else in their history, so I am very much identified with Wimbledon. But I am an American, and obviously the market here in the States was an even larger one for Wimbledon to shoot for. So I was the ideal bridge. Also, I had a commitment from NBC to be one of the announcers for Wimbledon, with the chance that I could further serve as a commentator for them with other sports, not only tennis. Perhaps even more important to me, Larry was starting to make it big as a promoter. He had put up with all that "Mr. Billie Jean King" junk through the years—and no one could have been better at it—but now, in his late thirties, like most any young business- man who had paid his dues, his career was starting to really take off—just as mine, the athlete's, was winding down.

I was so happy for him, and for me, and for so many people around me, and I was even seriously thinking again about how now might, at last, be the right time for me to have a baby, or for us to adopt one.

And then I came back to my room in Orlando, and there was one of those little pink phone messages with all the boxes to check—CALLED/PLEASE CALL were the two marked here. The message was from the Los Angeles *Times*, and it said they wanted to ask me about "the suit." That is how I found out that Marilyn Barnett had sued me.

All I knew at first was that I had to get away. I thought about a lot of places that I could run to, but at last I decided that I'd rather think things out in our apartment in New York. There was a night flight out from Orlando, so I bailed out on it.

I was stunned and hurt and angry. The suit came, at this moment, like a bolt out of the blue, even if I had known for some time that Marilyn's lawyer might well choose to sue. I had been certain there was potential trouble brewing for almost two years now, ever since I had heard through a friend, who was a customer at the hair salon where Marilyn worked, that Marilyn had boasted loudly that she had letters that I had written her and, "I could sell these for a lot of money." Marilyn had also threatened me with the letters on a couple of occasions.

I heard the same sort of report from Jim Jorgenson, my

business manager, sometime during the middle of 1979. As he would eventually testify at the trial: "I was talking to Marilyn about Billie Jean selling the house and Marilyn said: 'Why would Billie Jean want to hurt me that way? I have never hurt Billie Jean but I could hurt her and hurt her a lot.' "

Q: Did you ask her what she meant by that?

A: No, I pretty much knew.

Q: At that time of the summer, spring and summer of '79, were you aware that there had been letters from Mrs. King to Ms. Barnett?

A: Yes.

Q: And were you aware that Ms. Barnett still had the letters?

A: Yes.

Q: How were you made aware of that?

A: Marilyn told me.

Then, only a few weeks before the suit was actually filed, came the claims from her lawyer that I owed Marilyn a variety of things. For openers, she claimed that I had promised to support her for the rest of her life. This was such madness that when I first heard about it, I actually screeched into the phone. And now, more specifically, more immediately, Marilyn was ensconced in our house on the beach at Malibu—the one Jim referred to—and she wouldn't vacate. Naturally, she said that I had promised her that, too, in perpetuity.

Obviously, the normal procedure in any such dispute would be for the two parties to have a meeting and discuss the matter. That's why the suit, when it came, was so completely surprising, because no matter what the issues, I had always just assumed that Marilyn's lawyer—any lawyer—would first ask for a meeting and try to work things out before involving the courts. But when I got to New York, to our apartment, where I could be at peace with myself and think clearly, I could begin to sort things out better. I walked around that apartment for hours, in and out of rooms, almost the whole time holding a racket out and bouncing a ball up and down off it. It's wonderfully concentrating. And in my own mind I began to understand what was going on.

Marilyn had kept a number of letters that I had written her years before. As far as she was concerned, this gave her a cudgel to wave over my head. Jim Jorgenson, my business manager, had tried, without success, to get the letters back. And now it was becoming obvious: Marilyn and her lawyer assumed that I would do anything to make sure that she sat on the letters and kept them out of public scrutiny.

While I was thinking things over in New York, I was conferring, essentially, with four people over the phone. They were Larry, who was down in Florida on business; Pat Kingsley, my public-relations manager in Los Angeles; Dennis Wasser, my lawyer, who was also in Los Angeles; and Bob Kain, who represents me at International Management Group (IMG), the Mark McCormick organization in Cleveland. I told Larry first that, the more I thought about it, the more I thought that I ought to go public with my side, the truth of the matter.

"Whatever you want, Billie Jean," Larry said. He knew how impossible Marilyn had become.

"It's going to hurt you," I said. "And it's going to hurt my parents and a lot of people who are close to me. And it's going to hurt women's tennis, women's sports. But I really don't see how letting this thing come out in drips and drabs will be any better."

"Look, don't worry about other people," Larry said. "Just for once in your life do exactly what you want to do for yourself."

"Okay."

"No matter what happens, I'll take care of you, Billie Jean. The two of us can always get by."

"Wait a minute," I cried out. It's curious, but no matter

how bad things might be, you can always find something to laugh at. *"Get by!* I don't want to get by! I'm too old now. I still need my comforts."

And for the last time in a long time, we laughed.

Nothing was going to change my mind now. The others who I told my decision to were leery at first, but there was nothing they could say that convinced me otherwise. Because I was sure that the thing would never just go away of its own accord. It was always going to be there, nagging at us, and every time it might fade a little, we could be sure that Marilyn and her lawyer would do something to bring it back into the public eye.

Of course, not everybody agreed with my decision to speak out. One of the last people I reached, a close business associate, was flabbergasted.

"But why not?" I asked.

"Well, you know, it's just that no one's ever done anything like that before," he said.

"I don't care," I said. "Do you have any idea what the press will do with this? They'll chew me up and spit me out."

And I knew they would. I'm a certified controversial character, to start with—whatever that means, however you earn it. I represent certain images to certain people, and often what I represent is disliked. I hate labels so much, but they hang on me like a Christmas tree.

And anyway, all that aside, nothing seems to titillate the press and the public more than homosexuality—and particularly if it relates in any form to a female athlete, because we're all supposed to be gay. Right? I've known well enough about all the slander and innuendo applied to us. If I had been caught making love to a male movie star at high noon in Times Square, it wouldn't even make the six-o'clock news. But Billie Jean and another woman . . .

"Look," I went on, "whatever the consequences, I'm a person who takes risks. And the only way I can deal with this is to be aggressive and stand up. That's the way I am; that's the way I've always played tennis. Maybe it's safer the other way, but this is me, and I want to be true to myself."

At certain points in my life, once I make my mind up, there is just no sense in arguing with me. I can be a very stubborn person. In 1973, a couple of days before I played the famous Bobby Riggs match, when everything was absolutely set, when the world was waiting, I told Roone Arledge, who is the head of ABC Sports, that I was not going on the court if Jack Kramer was up there in the broadcast booth as one of the announcers. I have fought Kramer for what he stands against—women's tennis—all my life, and I wasn't going to have him up there on my coattails. And Arledge thought I was bluffing. I had told him how I felt about this for weeks, but he still thought it was all a little joke. But I didn't care if the whole human race had bet on that match, I was not going to play if Kramer was up there with Howard Cosell.

Finally, Arledge caught a glimmer. "You're not really serious, are you?" he asked.

Larry broke in. "Roone," he said, "Billie Jean won't play. She just won't. I know her. Don't force her to make that decision." Only then, at the eleventh hour, did Arledge ax Kramer.

And that's the way I was feeling now about what I had to do. I was going to stand up and speak out—and, if you will, take it like a man, whatever followed. I told my friends this: "Look, whatever happens in this thing, whatever I lose, I am determined not to lose my soul."

I had been completely holed up in my apartment. Dina Makarova, an interpreter I had met when we had traveled to Russia, who had subsequently taught me so much about ballet, came over and gave me some company. She'd go out and get me food. Now, when Larry and I left for Los Angeles, I took off my glasses to give me some kind of disguise, and we took a flight out of Newark instead of Kennedy. Meanwhile, in Los Angeles, Pat Kingsley was already starting to set the press conference up for the next morning, where I would look into the faces and the cameras and talk into the microphones and the tape recorders and admit, yes, I had had an affair while I was married, and it was with a woman.

2 ALWAYS ON THE CUSP

What troubled me a lot about the revelations was how this would affect the way people would remember me. I'm not, in fact, nearly as hung up on this immortality business as a lot of athletes. Bjorn Borg, for example, was only twenty-three or twenty-four before he was making no bones about how he wanted to go out: acknowledged as the best ever. Now Chris Evert Lloyd has picked up on that. She talks about it regularly in public, which is wise of her because you can't always depend on the press coming up with original notions. So Chrissie says she would like to go out as the best ever, that's what she's striving for, and the press writes that, and they start talking about her as potentially the greatest of all time, and that way she's got a chance to actually end up touted with that top ranking. You've got to win in sports—that's talent—but you've also got to learn how to remind everybody how you did win, and how often. That comes with experience.

But honestly, I've never cared that much for cementing my place in history. Sports is so transitory, so ephemeral. It just seems like so much nonsense comparing me to Helen Wills Moody or Suzanne Lenglen or anybody else from some other time. One lesson you learn from sports is that life goes on without you. As I recall, they didn't cancel the 1970 U.S. Open because I had to miss it on account of a knee operation. In 1973, when almost all the men boycotted Wimbledon, the controversy about their absence helped draw record crowds. There is always someone to put on tennis shoes and fill out the draw if you can't. It goes right on.

Still, what bothered me when I became aware that my privacy would be invaded and the affair would be publicly disclosed in the lawsuit was what people would think whenever my name came up. I feared that I always would be categorized by that, whatever else I have accomplished. I worked hard all of my life to achieve my goals. I will work hard to achieve future goals. I worked hard and became famous for being a tennis champion, and then, because of the disclosure, I was put in the vulnerable position of being remembered and categorized because of this very private and inconsequential episode.

The damage was compounded because the disclosure of my private affair surfaced when it did, right at the time when I was finishing as a player. Now, I have very little time left to play championship tennis to help people forget that insignificant part of my life. There is no way I can get back in the news for winning something on the tennis court, which could send the Marilyn episode back to oblivion. I do have some faith that the world is more understanding now. Still, I fear that, years ahead, when people hear the name of Billie Jean King, they will think of scandal before championships. And that would hurt, hurt very badly. I don't want that.

It worries me more, though, that public disclosure of the affair will come to reflect unfavorably upon women's tennis also. I fear that the sport is in for a hard three or four years.

Sponsors will drop women tennis players arbitrarily and without an afterthought. There are just so many worthwhile enterprises—sporting and otherwise—competing for sponsors' support these days, and so they might figure that they do not need anything which they think will create risk.

Most of the men in charge of sponsors' decisions are proud to call themselves conservatives, but I don't believe they are. To me, a conservative is supposed to be someone in favor of individual freedom. But these men will be the first to back away if someone they're associated with exercises that freedom. One of the first ramifications of my situation was that a prominent male corporation executive denied another woman an important public-relations position merely because *he heard* she was a lesbian.

In my case, too, I'm not just a player, not just an ex-champion, but I am, to many people, the personification of women's tennis. So I know very well that this distant episode in my life—one player's life—is going to give a great many nice folks the opportunity to categorize me and some other women tennis players as homosexuals. After all, aren't I the same outspoken women's libber who beat an old ex–world champion in the Astrodome? What can anyone expect from me, anyway?

I am a woman, however, and I will always be. I hope I can take about anything they throw at me—and not necessarily because I'm thick-skinned. But because, in a way, I've had a certain amount of practice at feeling uncomfortable. I've always had the feeling that I was different and that people were critical of that.

In many respects, I like being different. I also like being successful. I somehow always knew that I would succeed. I had a great sense of destiny from the time I was very young. I remember one incident so vividly. When I was only about five or six years old, I was standing with my mother in the kitchen at home in Long Beach. I told her flat out that when I grew up I was going to be the best at something. She just smiled and kept peeling potatoes or doing whatever it was she was doing. She said, "Yes, dear; yes, of course, dear," as if I had simply said that I was going to my room or going to eat an apple, or whatever.

So, I have always felt different that way. But it is also true that, as I got older, I could sense that I was different in other ways as well. Of course, I believe everyone is different in some way. I believe that people should not label anyone. I fear that people will tend to categorize me now because of the affair. That is wrong. That affair has nothing to do with my feelings, my perceptions of who I am and what I have done or what I want to do. That does not make me a misfit or anything else. I am still a woman. I am still an athlete.

Of course, much of the reason why I've always felt that I was out of place was because of sports. First, a girl who wanted to excel in athletics was considered to be strange. In the second place, it was all a hopeless dream, anyhow. I think I began to appreciate this when I was only eight or nine, when my father took me to see the old Los Angeles Angels play the Hollywood Stars in the Triple-A Pacific Coast League at Wrigley Field in L.A. (The Stars were especially memorable. They wore short pants.)

Right away, I loved it, but it was unfair of me to love it, I understood soon enough, because there was no place for an American girl to go in the *national* pastime. This all came back to me when I saw a commercial on television recently and a whole bunch of kids, boys and girls alike, are all climbing out of a station wagon or getting hamburgers or doing something fun together, and they're all dressed up in baseball uniforms. I'm sure that most people who watch this commercial think how forward it is, how progressive, showing girls on the team, girls in uniform just like the boys. And I have such mixed emotions about that commercial. It's great that they include girls, but at the same time it's cruel because all it can possibly do is make some little girl somewhere wrongly think that she can be a baseball player, too. And of course she can't. There is no life for girls in team sports past Little League.

I got into tennis when I realized this, and because I thought golf would be too slow for me, and I was too scared to swim. What else could a little girl do if she wasn't afraid to sweat? But as good as I was, and as much as I loved tennis right from the start, I found myself out of place there, too, because it was a country-club game then, and I came from a working-class family. My father was a fireman, and we didn't have any money for rackets, much less for proper tennis dresses. The first time I was supposed to be in a group photograph was at the Los Angeles Tennis Club during the Southern California Junior Championships. They wouldn't let me pose because I was only able to wear a blouse and a pair of shorts that my mother had made for me. All the other players were photographed.

I had some physical defects also. I had bad eyes—20/400—in a sport where nobody wore glasses. And, even as quick and as fast as I've been, I've been fat all over at times, with chubby little legs, and there are railroad tracks on both my knees from a number of knee operations. All that has been very apparent, but perhaps what has made it even more difficult for me as an athlete is my breathing problem. I inherited sinus trouble from my mother and chest problems from my father. The worst times of all for me have been in England, where I've played my very best and set all those records. I don't think there was one year at Wimbledon when I was entirely well. I always had a problem breathing there. I guess I am nearly a physical wreck. You see, nothing about me is quite what it seems.

People mischaracterized me even before the affair. I am supposed to be tough, loud, brash, and insensitive. In fact, Larry says I am very shy, and I really dislike being in the company of more than five or six people. I'm really a one-on-

one person. So many people thought I was scared and crumbling under the pressure before the Bobby Riggs match. There happened to be a regular women's tournament in Houston that same week, and I was forced to play in it if I played Riggs—can you imagine the best players today getting that treatment?—and so, one day, without warning, I showed up in the locker room, and almost every player there was scrambling to bet against me. Rosie Casals was the only one backing me. That really hurt, that they didn't have any faith in me.

I had warned Margaret Court when she first told me that she had signed to play Riggs (for $10,000—she thought that was big money) that she was going to have to deal with a whole *season*—not just a day's match. So I knew the buildup would be even greater for Bobby's and my match; we were working off the Court–Riggs momentum. We signed on July 11 for the September 20 showdown, and the hype never really stopped. If it started to slow down, Bobby would whip it back up again.

So all along, my main strategy was not to get swept along in the promotion. Just because I was half of the show on court didn't mean I had to be part of the warm-up act, too. As much as possible, and right up to curtain time, I tried to stay out of the hoopla. After all, it wasn't as if I was needed to sell tickets and hustle the television. We drew 30,472 to the Astrodome and 40,000,000 American TV viewers—plus millions more abroad—so it did well enough without my becoming another carnival barker. Bobby was quite good enough at that.

Nothing he did surprised me. The reception was very much what I expected, and it didn't faze me. I'd played arenas before, and the circus atmosphere Bobby created just made it all of a piece. The only fear I did have was when they brought me in on the litter like Cleopatra. I don't like heights and I was afraid that they were going to drop me. But even my gift of the pig to Bobby and his gift of the big Sugar Daddy to me passed immediately out of my mind. I was really concentrating on my strategy.

The thing that I thought was especially important going in was to volley well. Obviously, I wanted to hit every shot well, and I planned in practice to play an all-court game, sometimes at the net, sometimes back. But I knew Bobby felt that women were poor players at the net, and when I had seen the tape of the Court match, it was apparent that she had reinforced this opinion by playing so badly at net—on those rare occasions when she could get up there. So, to me, it would be psychologically telling if Riggs suddenly realized that this woman could volley.

And I did, too. Five of the first six times he tried to pass me with his backhand, I volleyed away winners. He had me down a service break at 3–2, but by then I knew I could take the net at will, and when I broke right back, that pretty much told the tale. Oh sure, almost right to the end there were all those people who thought Bobby fell behind only to get better odds on his courtside bets, but as far as I was concerned, almost from the first I was amazed at how weak an opponent he really was. All I ever feared was the unknown, and soon enough he was a known quantity for me.

That match was such madness. How often in this world can you suddenly have something which is altogether original and yet wonderfully classic? And what could be more classic than the battle of the sexes? The only problem for me is that I think everybody else in the world—Bobby included—had more fun with that match than I did. Men's tennis would not suffer if Bobby lost, so he had nothing to lose.

Perhaps people would have known how much it all mattered to me if they could have seen an incident a few days before.

I was practicing down in South Carolina, and I came in for a snack. Dick Butera, my friend, the owner of the Philadelphia Freedoms of World Team Tennis and the husband of

Julie Anthony, another friend, was lying on the floor, watching a college football game. It was halftime, and the Stanford band was entertaining, and suddenly, as I watched, the band began playing "I Am Woman," and then I realized that they had formed my initials, BJK, on the field, and Dick looked up to share this moment with me, and we both had tears in our eyes. I think that was the happiest the Riggs match ever made me.

But it was never the match itself that upset me. It was all the people clamoring after me. My whole life, I wanted to have mobs of people cheer for tennis, but I really become quite frightened when everybody pushes around me and wants to touch me. I hate it when strangers touch me, even though I understand it is almost always for love, and that they don't mean anything harmful. Still, at the time, when it happens, it scares me.

I have often been asked whether I am a woman or an athlete. The question is absurd. Men are not asked that. I am an athlete. I am a woman. I want all other women to have their rights, because above all else, I'm for individual freedom, but there is very much about the goals and the methods of the women's movement that I disagree with. That is the refusal to recognize that both men and women view each other through sexual bias. Oh, I know this is going to get me in trouble, but I'm going to mention it anyway. I've got a male friend in business, and he told me once that he'd really rather have a good-looking, well-built blonde who can barely manage as his secretary than some old lady who is a secretarial whiz. That's his privilege, I think. And if the blonde takes the job knowing that she's going to get leered at and chased around the desk, fair enough.

I'm still not even absolutely convinced that we need the Equal Rights Amendment. If it means the end of discrimination on the basis of gender, then I want it. But I don't believe you can legislate people's minds. I believe that it is persuasion you need, not force. Just because you legislate does not mean that people will change. This reminds me of what happened in the waning days of the Roman Empire. Initially, citizenship in the Empire had been one of the most highly prized possessions, but this changed as the Roman Empire began to legislate people's values and behavior patterns. The legislation reached such an extent that in the last days of the empire, Roman citizens were renouncing their citizenship in order to come under the more relaxed alien laws. Citizenship had come to be considered more of a burden than a prize. People simply had become fed up with so much legislation. As another example, there are some countries where people are leaving in droves because of heavy taxation, lack of personal freedom, and overly protective legislation. I do not want that to happen to us.

Sometimes the women's movement reminds me too much of some organized religion, which I can't stand. I was very (quote) religious (unquote) as a kid. Also, I was much less tolerant then. That seems to me to be the trouble with movements, be they Women's Liberation or the Moral Majority or whatever. Then you always have to be against somebody on every issue, and I'm not very good at that. I don't like confrontations. But, of course, I always performed my best when the confrontation was most heightened, in the clutch—the most well-known example being the Riggs match. Nothing ever really fits for me.

I was a virgin when I was supposed to be, and I got married to the right cute boy the way I was supposed to at the time I was supposed to, but then we only had a "normal" marriage for a couple years—or, anyway, what most Americans presume a normal marriage to be, even if that ideal barely exists anymore. I never feel comfortable with a lot of so-called "normal" married people because they seem threatened by the way Larry and I live—and this was the case even long before people knew about my affair with Marilyn and could say "I told you so" instead of just "I'll bet she's queer." So I've never really felt at home in that huge world of married people, but I've also never felt at all comfortable when I've been associated with the gay world. Maybe it's mostly that everybody wants reinforcement of their kind of life, and I don't provide that for anybody.

I guess I'm just very much a loner. Except for one thing: I really can't stand to be alone for long. Sometimes I ask myself, Billie Jean, where do you belong? Do you fit in anywhere? Maybe all my life I've just been trying to change things so there would be someplace right for me.

I think the sense—the fear?—of not belonging is greater in my particular case, too, because the ground has kept shifting under my feet. I was born on the cusp—Scorpio/Sagittarius, November 22; John Kennedy was shot on my twentieth birthday—and maybe that set the stage for my life. In a way, it seems that I've lived on the cusp for a long time, because everywhere, as I approached something, it turned, it changed. Nothing really happened as I had plotted it.

Any woman born around 1943 has had to endure so many changes—in her educational experience, in her working life, in sex, in her roles, her expectations. But with me, it always seemed that I was also on the cutting edge of that change. Any woman about my age—or, for that matter, any person who has had to deal with women, which is just about everybody— has been a part of a great social transition, and just to survive that intact has been an accomplishment for me. I was brought up in a very structured universe—in my family, in school, in tennis, in every part of my world. Then, all of a sudden, the rules all started to change, and it seemed there weren't any rules left. I tried to go with the flow, but always seemed to find myself out in front and on the line.

When I married Larry in 1965, we were going to have babies—lots of them, as far as I was concerned—and I was going to give up tennis, which is the way it was supposed to be. In fact, only two weeks after we were married, I thought I was pregnant. And I was delighted. But even when I found out

I wasn't having a baby, I was happy enough just spending so much time with Larry. I'd cook him two meals at home every day and take him his lunch—even when he was on the night shift—to the factory where he worked making ice cream cartons.

As for tennis, it hardly mattered. There certainly wasn't any career for me there. It was just fun, and in those days, before professionals were accepted in the main tournaments, there was no money to speak of. We amateurs—"shamateurs" was the accepted term—took what we could in the way of "expenses" under the table, and if it wasn't much, it was still like found money to a young couple, and it helped Larry through law school.

I won Wimbledon three years running, and outside the little tennis community, very few people knew. In 1967 I won all three titles at Wimbledon—singles, doubles, and mixed— and I came back to my country, and there was no one there to meet me, no one at all. And barely six years later, there I was, in the Houston Astrodome, playing prime time to the world in what amounted to the Roman Colosseum, with everyone in civilization chanting my name, hating me or loving me. And everyone wanted—needed—part of me, for tennis or move- ments or friendship or politics or just for the hell of it— Wouldja, couldja, canya, Billie Jean?—and people were throwing money at me or grabbing at me or calling me a symbol or a leader or a radical feminist. I didn't know where I was. It was so complicated, and one morning I woke up, and where was I? I was in another woman's bed.

So now I know a lot of people will call me a homosexual, but to me that's just another label. As I said, I cannot stand categorization. I'm not concerned for me. I just don't want Larry and my parents and my brother and the other people who love me hurt. And maybe now I can spend some time carving out a place for me in the world around me instead of only in the record books.

3 DOUBLE WHAMMY

The pressure really began building on me in 1971. That was the first full year of the Virginia Slims tour, and I was not only the best player for the Slims but the drawing card as well, and because I worked comfortably with the press I pretty much became the first line of public relations, too. That was the year I went over $100,000 in prize money for the first time, which, from a blunt point of view, was no big deal—Rod Laver made $292,000 on the men's tour that same year—but it was very symbolic that a woman athlete exceeded that benchmark, so I went for it, never letting up.

For that matter, whether I intended it so or not, almost everything I did was defined as symbolic. And the battles continued in 1972, when I found myself leading the fight against the USLTA's competitive women's tour and battling the U.S. Open for prize money equal to what the men were being allotted. I have never been the same since 1972. Those couple years were so intense. I just gave, gave, gave, and afterward there was something that just wasn't there for me to draw on anymore. Neither my motivation nor my energy level has ever been quite so high again.

If only it had been a matter of hard work, of going through the motions, it would have been long and tedious, but it would not all have consumed me in the way it did. Making women's sports acceptable, and making women's tennis, particularly, into a legitimate big-league game was a crusade for me, and I threw my whole self into it in ways that exhausted me emotionally as much as they did physically.

It is my tendency, anyway, to focus too completely on what I'm involved with at any one time. As Larry, who knows me best of all, has told me, "Billie Jean, you demand total attention, and whatever you're dealing with, you take everything out of it and pour all of yourself in." I do that if I'm talking to a maître d' while I'm waiting for a table. I do that with locker-room attendants. So you can imagine how much of myself I gave to a crusade that meant so much of my whole life to me.

Week after week we were on the road, often out of the country, and every day that I was not traveling was much the same: promoting, practicing, playing, then talking some more to the press. I can remember starting magazine interviews after midnight because that was the only time left to get them in. And then I'd have to be up for some early-morning TV show. The apartment that Larry and I have in New York is on the West Side, near Columbus Circle, and there's a little greasy spoon nearby, and I don't ever pass it when I'm out walking when I don't remember getting a bite of breakfast there because it was the only place open in the neighborhood at the early hour of the morning we were up for TV. It was five-thirty, quarter to six—something like that—and we were going to appear on some show with a host named John Bartholomew Tucker.

It was Rosie Casals, Ann Jones and her husband, Pip, and me, and it was all so depressing. The Dawn Patrol! And I was the one who wanted to quit, right there. The others had to encourage me. "Billie Jean, you're the born leader—you have to," Ann said.

It wasn't either that I just had to meet with the press all the time. Answering questions can be easy. But most of the press people we had to deal with hadn't the foggiest idea about tennis, much less about women's tennis, and so, effectively, it was a matter of having to help them with the questions so then you could give them the answers. The ones who knew a little bit about us were the worst because they inclined to be smug and condescending: "What are you girls really trying to do?"—that sort of thing. Believe me, it was incredibly wearing. In many respects, playing the matches was the easiest part.

Larry and I, and our marriage, really suffered. It was one of those horrible cases where it seemed we had to choose between our dreams and ourselves. There is no question, looking back, that our dreams were hurting us. I was always so tired and so lonely, and I wanted Larry with me so much, but I couldn't ask him to come along with me—like, for example, Pip traveled with Ann. Larry simply is not the kind of person who could trail after me from tournament to TV studio to airport to hotel. He had tried it once and it didn't work. He had his own career and goals. For that matter, as dedicated as he was, too, to the future of women's tennis, there was more he could do for the sport working back in California and he did just that. Do you get the picture? If I asked Larry to be with me, for me, I was hurting him and tennis—and, ultimately, us—even more. I'm told that's what psychologists call a double bind. I always called it a double whammy.

In February of 1971, in Boston, when Larry came to watch me play in the indoors, I got pregnant. It was the first time and the only time, but I knew right away. I had just gone off the pill because of some complications, but I was pretty regular, and I thought we were okay. Was I wrong. I swear, I knew it the next morning.

Larry and I had a great deal of discussion about what I would do. First of all, it was strictly my choice because Larry is not the kind of guy who merely pays lip service to certain popular feminist beliefs. He totally accepts the notion that a woman's body is her own, and so for him it was altogether up to me to decide what I wanted to do. I told him I wanted an abortion.

I can't imagine that any woman *wants* to get an abortion, that anyone enjoys it, and even though I never considered for a moment that I might be killing some human—because I was only five weeks along—it was still an agonizing experience for me. In those days, too, you had to apply for approval for your abortion to a committee of doctors. It was so degrading. Then, the day I actually had the abortion, I sat almost all the time, in my hospital gown, with a young black girl from Alabama who was in her fifth or sixth month—her boyfriend long since disappeared. After being with her, I never again had any doubts about the fact that abortion is a matter of individual choice.

Of course, it was traumatic, and a lot of that involved Larry because I know how much he loves children—he's the one who brought up our dog, Lucy—and he would have adored a baby. Later, when it was revealed that I had had an abortion, everybody who either dislikes me or disapproves of abortion—and it's fair to say that there is an awful lot of overlapping in those two groups—jumped to the conclusion that I had given up on the baby because it might conflict with the convenience of my playing tennis. In fact, that consideration never so much as crossed my mind—not once. The only thing I really thought about was our marriage, and I concluded that it wasn't very solid at that particular time. It's funny; we were so dedicated to so many dreams, but even though most of them were shared, we didn't have the time to share each other, and we were drifting apart. And so I concluded that this was no time to bring a child into the King family. I had the abortion in Berkeley, near where we were living at the time, and two days later I was on my way to Florida to play in a tournament because they needed me there.

For the next year or so, while nothing improved in our married life, the professional demands increased all the more. It was at the time when Bobby Riggs first started bugging me to play him, but I didn't even give that a serious thought. Women's tennis was starting to take off; the last thing we needed was a sideshow. In fact, women's tennis was coming along so well that I should have been able somehow to have traded off the values in my mind—been able to accept less success in sports while maintaining my marriage. But two things prohibited this. First of all, I have such high expectations. Not only at that time but even to this day, I still don't think that tennis—never mind women's tennis—has succeeded all that much. So it was not exactly as if I thought my dreams were fulfilled, my life's work done.

And secondly, I still loved Larry King—he was so incredibly understanding of me—and I knew that he loved me. I was not very happy; I had to find myself.

The first time I met Marilyn Barnett was in May of 1972. She was a hairdresser in Beverly Hills, at Gene Shacove's, a very well-known salon in Los Angeles. One of the players, Tory Fretz, recommended Marilyn when I mentioned in the locker room that I needed to have my hair done, and so I made an appointment. Marilyn struck me as a nice person, but she made more of an initial impression on me for the good job she did on my hair.

I ran into her again sometime that summer or fall, when I came back to Los Angeles again. By then I had won the French, won Wimbledon, won Forest Hills. I was twenty-eight years old, and I was at the height of my powers. I'm quite sure I could have won the Grand Slam that year, 1972, but the Australian was such a minor-league tournament at that time, and it was scheduled then in January of 1973, before I knew I would win the Big Three. More important, I did not want to miss any Virginia Slims winter tournaments. I was playing enough as it was. In fact, I was so tired at the end that the last tournament I played that year was in Florida, and after I lost two and four to Chrissie, Larry took me right back to California, and everybody was afraid that I had mononucleosis.

But I didn't have any diagnosable disease. I was just plain worn out. The more I had won that year, the less it meant in a way, and the more tired and sad I became. And the more I won, the more people wanted a part of me. I will tell you King's First Law of Recognition: You never get it when you want it, and then when it comes, you get too much.

Always groups, always mobs, always parties. I could never be alone with Larry. It was at a friend's house when I saw Marilyn again. She laughed and asked me when I was coming back to have my hair done again, and it was so very casual, so relaxed, and that is the way it started. The next time I saw her, a couple days later, it was just the two of us, taking it easy, up at her place on Doheny Drive, which she rented at the time.

Marilyn is small and blond, with a little, birdlike voice. She struck me as a nice person, easily affectionate, and simple. In fact, I was really astonished at the claims in her suit that she was my "sole confidante," that I divulged things to her that I never told anyone else. Even at the height of our affair, I never told Marilyn anything important. What I liked most about her was that I could escape from everything when I was with her. That was the whole point: *not* to involve her in all that had me in turmoil. It was suddenly wonderful that after a full day of problems and confusion I could just go up to Marilyn's place and collapse.

And then, before too long, I realized that something was

different, that I seemed to be falling in love with Marilyn. At first I just couldn't understand. I could not comprehend how this could be happening—and strangest of all, here I was apparently falling in love with a woman.

Of course, I continued to question myself, especially when the relationship became physical, which was soon enough. I knew well enough there were lesbians in tennis, and I also knew well enough that some of the public tends to assume that almost all female athletes are lesbians, but I had certainly never dwelt on the subject of homosexuality before. The gays and straights and bisexuals on tour coexist wonderfully and it's no big deal. The last thing that crossed my mind these nights was whether or not my actions might someday have an impact on women's tennis.

Growing up, I was conditioned to be leery of homosexuals, although I was not. I have always believed that sexual preferences are irrelevant; it is the total being that matters. The subject didn't come up at home much, and usually when it did my father would put a quick end to it. He had very strong—and I mean *very strong*—feelings about homosexuals. That was pretty much the prevailing view about homosexuals in the world I came from.

But by the time I started up with Marilyn, I had come to know some gays, and to understand them better, and I always spoke up for gay rights. Still, it was very significant to me at that time that Marilyn and I were only having an isolated homosexual experience, and that we were not participating in a full homosexual life-style, because I'll admit that that insular, segregated way of living puts me off a little. It did then, and it still does. But understand: a typical heterosexual, suburban life-style also is not right for me.

It is important to keep me in perspective, and to remember the massive changes that I was experiencing at this time. My whole world was in flux. In one way, Marilyn was a safe harbor for me, but in another she was like a storm at sea, swamping me. Particularly once we started to have sex, I remember how much it meant to me that Marilyn had been living with a man right up to the time we fell in love. That was very important to me. I can't stand women who don't like men. I don't care if they don't want to sleep with them, but imagine writing off half the human race.

At my press conference, when I first spoke up about all this, I made the remark "I don't feel homosexual," and that angered some gays, I know, because it could be construed to sound as if I were denying what I had done. But that wasn't at all what I intended. I meant only that I had never lived as a homosexual, in that full life-style, and that when I had the relationship with Marilyn I felt no differently than I ever have. Obviously I must be bisexual. I suspect many people are, only they're not aware of it. I couldn't have sustained the affair with Marilyn and not be bisexual.

But the point I was trying to make was that I felt no differently with Marilyn than I did when I made love to a man. My point then was, as ever: please, no labels.

Obviously, I feel very differently about Marilyn now, but no matter how much she tried to damage me, no matter how much the trial took out of my life—and even if we did win a total victory—no matter how she betrayed me, I cannot pretend that I didn't love Marilyn Barnett once, in my own way. It was all so easy and uncomplicated with her, so different from the rest of my life. She didn't even know anything about sports. She made everything even smoother, too, by figuring out what I wanted and playing up to that. Being with her was a retreat for me. I never felt so soft and feminine in all my life as those months when I was having the affair with Marilyn.

In fact, I even had to laugh on one occasion shortly after all the news came out, when I was playing a match and some heckler screamed out, "Hey, take it easy on her, Billie Jean. She's only a girl." And I called back at the guy, "Don't worry, Marilyn was the aggressive one." I was the girl.

Yes, of course, I felt guilty. In the best Old Testament

tradition from my childhood, I felt fire-and-brimstone-sinful.
I felt all those things. I was cheating on my husband, and I
loved him. That was the one time in all my life when I really
let my heart run away with my head. But I'll tell you, I never
thought it made any difference what sex Marilyn happened to
be. To me, an affair is an affair, regardless.

Most people, when they hear that, don't agree with me at
all. Men, it seems, would much rather have their wife select
another man as a lover. I think, myself, that if a certain man
had come along at that time and if he was of a personality
much like Marilyn's, well, possibly I would have drifted into
an affair with him. I don't know. I do know that I kept it in the
back of my head at the time that, from a practical point of
view, I was better off with another woman because people
wouldn't be so likely to surmise what was happening. And
that was about the only practical thought I ever had then.

And after a while I didn't worry about that anymore. What
I kept thinking about, more and more, was how this lesbianism was supposed to be so different, and it wasn't. It wasn't,
at all. I guess it's only that love is much the same, whoever is
involved, and that it isn't the gender so much as the individuals, and that sex is just another way of communicating.

Not long after Marilyn sued and the affair became public, I
got a wonderful letter from Gloria Steinem, and here is much
of it:

Dearest Billy Jean,

We [*Ms.* magazine] once published an article, an excerpt
from a book that is yet to be published, about a study done
by two women psychologists. Instead of interviewing people on the subject of sexuality at only one point in time,
they were doing interviews over a lengthy period; about
four years.

The results, of course, were that couples who were completely heterosexual in year one had split up, with one

partner becoming gay or lesbian in year three. And people who said they were totally gay or lesbian in year two were sometimes married with kids in year four. In other words, it made clear that sexuality was a form of human expression as well as a way of procreating. . . . It was impossible not to see that sexuality is a continuum of expression for many or most people (probably for all of us potentially) and not just one box that we're artificially put into.

Until the day of such understanding comes, we're all going to be damaged and limited by labels. It breaks my heart to see you suffering or penalized in any way for living in a still unenlightened time, but please know your troubles have probably hastened a better understanding for everyone. Even the biased folks won't be able to think in such limited ways because someone they love and admire has been honest. It's not fair that you were forced into this position—but now that it's happened, I think some good will come of it. . . .

At the time Marilyn came into my life, I needed some release. I needed someone to love me in the way I needed to be loved. I still don't know if I needed to be away from Larry or away from the pressure. I just know that that was the way it was for me then. And I do know this too, and it really baffled me at the time, but even when I was with Marilyn, I was always still in love with Larry. People say that isn't possible, but all I can say is that that is the way it was for me, and even, as a matter of fact, the more I was with Marilyn, the more my love for Larry started to grow, too. Perhaps it was that the affair made it possible for me to like myself more, and so soon I felt it was time for me to devote more of myself to Larry.

4 "THIS WOULD MAKE A GREAT BOOK"

The intense part of my affair with Marilyn extended only for about a year. I read somewhere that that's about the typical run for an extramarital affair. The most expressive, personal letters—"the good ones"—all were written in that early period, at the end of 1972 and the beginning of '73.

Of course, a lot of people are dying to know why I wrote all those letters to Marilyn. As nearly as I can tell, as far as much of America is concerned, the lesson to learn from Billie Jean King is *not:* Don't cheat on your spouse. Instead, it is: If you do, don't write letters. I guess I felt the need to communicate my feelings to someone who I felt I was in love with. However, to this day, I still don't know for sure.

My main problem, I guess, is that I was an innocent in this game. I've always thought of myself as MOR—middle-of-the-road—when it comes to sex; I've neither been promiscuous nor preoccupied with the subject. So I suppose when I suddenly found myself in the middle of an affair, it was easy for me to let my enthusiasm overshadow my common sense. Looking back, I know that I was altogether sincere in my relationship. Also, looking back, I wonder what in the world made me think as I did. For me, it becomes only the ultimate proof of how different we all can be at different times in our lives—and especially in frantic times.

So, why did I write all the letters? Well, I was away a lot. And Marilyn asked me to write her. I am so distressed now by all that she has done to me, that it makes me wonder if even then she was plotting to entrap me. She's a good actress; and as naive as I was in many respects, I suppose it was quite easy for her to con me. So I would write her. And even if she initially had to ask me to write, I must admit that soon enough I warmed to the task. I loved writing Marilyn. I needed someone I could focus on, and I was pleased to have a new way to express myself.

The letters were never enough for Marilyn, though. Almost from the first she wanted me to bring her along as a companion. "Please take me with you," she would beg me. "I'm tired of being a hairdresser." And finally, in the spring of '73, I agreed, but only on the stipulation that she would come along as an employee at $600 a month. I hate freeloaders; I didn't want her to come along just for the ride. I was thinking about hiring a traveling secretary to help me out. So Marilyn quit her job as a hairdresser and began working full-time for me as my secretary, assistant, buffer, gofer—just general all-around Ms. Friday.

I think a lot of people in tennis are under the impression that she worked for me for many years, but the fact is that it was only about a year. I went back and checked the records carefully. Marilyn was especially visible, though, because she worked for me in 1973, at the time in my career when I had the most exposure—those months leading up to the Riggs match, when the whole world was interested in me.

If it had merely been a normal, run-of-the-mill, hectic, chaotic, pressure-packed year, then maybe it could have all worked out. Possibly, under more normal circumstances, she could have traveled along with me and our relationship would have just naturally, and painlessly, turned from one of lovers to one of two good friends. But it never really had that chance because Marilyn is, by nature, such a possessive person, and because, at that time, with all the Riggs activity building, she happened to be in the perfect position to exercise her possessiveness.

Actually, in the beginning, when she first went on the road with me, she performed her assignments capably enough. But soon enough problems arose. She spent too much of my money. The tips! If she wanted a pack of cigarettes, and we were in a hotel, she'd just call down and have room service send up a pack—payment and tip on the bill. Worse, soon she started unnecessarily barring people from getting to see me. Obviously, part of her job was to make sure that I got some privacy, but very quickly Marilyn turned that assignment into one whereby my privacy was defined as seeing no one except Marilyn Barnett. It wasn't just that she would screen my phone calls. If she knew the person calling me and didn't like him or her—which was just about everybody who knew me—then she would tell them that I wasn't available and refuse to pass the message along to me.

A few friends tried to let me know what was happening, but I was sure they were exaggerating or that Marilyn had just been overzealous in guarding me in their particular case. And anyway, I was defensive about Marilyn because I was still having an affair with her, but I was turning cool, and I recognized that, and I didn't want to hurt her. Also, this was long before I understood the most obvious truth, that in my opinion, Marilyn is a real conniver.

Early on, Marilyn had suggested that I should leave Larry—divorce him. At the time I accepted this as a perfectly natural response, what any "other woman" would say. It took me a long while, however, to appreciate that Marilyn didn't want me just to divorce Larry. She didn't like any of my friends. She wanted me to divorce everyone I had ever known and loved.

By the same token, it was also vital to her self-esteem for her to let the world know that we were a couple. I'm told that whenever she was working as a hairdresser, she couldn't wait to tell some of her customers that we were lovers—and never mind whether or not the customer cared at all about Billie Jean King. Now, of course, I can see that she was an opportunist, but at the time I failed to understand that; I hadn't gotten beneath her shell.

Larry, of course, remained unaware of the affair. The first real inkling he might have had came in the summer of 1978, when it initially became apparent that Marilyn might cause trouble. I told Larry, "Look, Marilyn's giving me a problem about something, but please don't ask me about it." And he didn't.

I know that some people were surprised by how evenly Larry continued to comport himself when the affair became public knowledge. In fact, I've heard that a few people have even assumed he must be gay—which, I can, just for the record, promise you is ridiculous. Larry is simply a very composed person, and very compassionate, and when at last he knew the truth, he came to grips with it in his way, true to himself.

Maybe the best way to explain Larry's thought processes is to relate the conversation that Frank Deford had with him when he was beginning to help me prepare this book. When Larry told him about his ability to accept other people's choices, Frank replied, "But Larry, as beautiful a sentiment as that is, you're human, too. What about your happiness? At some point doesn't your wife's right to happiness impinge upon you, so that it makes you unhappy?"

"Possibly. But you must understand that I'm a very secure person—much more secure than Billie Jean, for example. I have a great deal more inner security than she does. She needs to obtain that sort of assurance from the outside—from the crowds, the press, whatever. At least to some extent. But I am totally secure within myself, and because of that, I think I'm always happy."

"Always?"

"I have *never* been unhappy," Larry replied. "Never. And by the same token, I know that Billie Jean is the sort of person who is never going to permit herself to be totally happy. Long before Marilyn Barnett came into Billie Jean's life, we knew where we stood with each other. And remember, it's a two-way street: I exasperate Billie Jean in many ways simply because we are such different personalities."

"And she exasperates you, too?"

"Not really. Because I'm the sort of person who can better accept people for what they are. Billie Jean never gives up trying to make me adjust in some way, to open up more, for example. But that's impossible, because it's just not me. But it never stops her from trying to make me over in some way. So I back away. My ego is not in the way, either, because I don't want to possess her."

To me, this is an illustration of Larry's great strength. But, of course, some people see it the other way around. I am astonished to find out, for example, that there are people who are surprised to discover that Larry is not leaving me because of the affair. But to him, that is something over and done with, and he is only upset now that Marilyn became so spiteful.

So, you see, that is Larry. A great many people talk a good game, but he is really true to his philosophy. And don't be misled into thinking that he is a real pushover; he acts not without some human nature. Larry knows that if he is tolerant of me, then he can anticipate that I'll give him a lot more room, too. I have to laugh because recently we have been arguing about his learning to fly helicopters in Hawaii. When Larry makes up his mind, it is almost impossible to dissuade him. And now, I have to admit, after I've seen him in action, flying a copter, I like it. It's great for him.

Anyway, when the Riggs match was finally over and that hullabaloo began to die down, I took that as a polite excuse and told Marilyn that I really didn't need her as a constant traveling companion any longer. Besides, just as I didn't need her help as a secretary, neither did I love her anymore either. Both the physical and romantic aspects of our relationship had cooled considerably. I still cared for Marilyn, though, but I was beginning to learn more and more about how much she had lied, about how much she had misused the authority I had given her, about how much, in effect, she had abused me.

Finally, in the spring of 1974, I told her I would have to let her go. She said she would return to being a hairdresser. Marilyn had always told me that she was alone in the world, without any real family except for one stepbrother. In fact, this was a complete fiction, and even the "stepbrother" was a full-blooded sibling—but it was after the lawsuit before I found out that she really did have family.

In any event, at the time, I did feel sorry for her, and so I made an arrangement to provide some sort of severance pay for her, and I agreed that she could stay in the beach house at Malibu for a while, until Larry and I decided otherwise. In fact, I made it plain at the time that Marilyn would have to pay us rent—$120 a month—maintain and protect the property, and be in charge of helping remodel the main house and the tiny little guest house that was also on the property.

I thought this would provide some stability to her life, and it was important to me that she not be on the cuff, that she be paying for the privilege of living there. It is also true that Larry and I were not exactly real-estate moguls at the time. In fact, we were in no ways rich. People hear "Malibu" and "beach house," and, I know, right away they imagine great potentates living in opulence. It was hardly that way. At the time we bought the house in 1973 for $132,500 our total worth was less than $100,000. The house was, it turned out, a very wise investment, but it was also a very careful one. We also wanted to purchase another piece of property in Orange County at that time, but we simply didn't have the where-withal.

Soon enough Marilyn stopped paying rent. I don't remember how that came about in the first place; however, when I understood the situation, I let it pass. I was just too generous. It's simply not my nature to tell anybody to shove it, especially someone who had been as dear to me as Marilyn. I suppose my friend Teddy Tinling, the fashion designer, is correct when he says that the Scorpio in me shows in such situations, when I haunch up and end up stinging myself. I sure did in this case. It was just easier for me to put the thing out of my mind and hope that it—and Marilyn—would somehow fade away. As I said, I hate confrontations. I will do absolutely anything to avoid one off the tennis court. In fact, I've thought sometimes that the reason I've done so well in tennis, especially in the clutch, in the crucial matches, is that I can channel all my combative instincts to the court and direct those energies into my game. I don't dissipate any of that in the everyday world.

It's hard to pinpoint times, but I believe it must have been early in '75, sometime after Marilyn moved in at Malibu, when she started to connive. There's a lot of detail I forget because I saw so little of her. Marilyn liked to give the impression that we were constantly together, but, in fact, we spent little time with each other after the spring of 1974. In her depositions for the trial, she referred, for example, to endless days we had with each other, when we were apart only when I went onto the court, but some of these 24-hour days she said we shared together in Malibu were when Larry and I were living together across the continent, in Philadelphia, when I played World Team Tennis with the Freedoms.

After 1974 I would, in fact, only occasionally spend time with her in Malibu. Usually, when I did, it would be for two or three days; I would go out there and just collapse—read, watch TV, sleep, get away from it all. Marilyn would cook for us then. She makes out that this proves she was some kind of surrogate housewife, but in fact, she loved to cook. That was one thing she really enjoyed doing.

I did see a little more of her in '77 than the previous years, but this was not so much because I wanted to be with her, but because I was trying to help her by now. She pleaded with me that spring, so I brought her over to England, to Eastbourne, and then to the first week of the Wimbledon fortnight. That fall, too, she came with me when I played in Puerto Rico. I remember the English trip especially well, in retrospect, because it does provide one clear benchmark in my mind. Marilyn wanted to make love then, and we were no longer making love. So I know for certain that all that had ended absolutely before the summer of '77.

It was the next summer, though, when things really began to blow up. That was when I told Marilyn that we were planning to sell the house, and when she first began to threaten me. I specifically recall one horrible day in that August of '78 when she was at our apartment in New York. I was with my traveling secretary, Ron McCabe. It was horrible. It is so funny that I have forgotten about every important tennis match in my life, but I can still hear absolutely in my mind the quiet click of the door as Ron left the apartment when Marilyn and I started arguing.

Later on, things got even worse. To spite me, on one occasion, Marilyn started taking what appeared to be drugs right in front of me. I asked her not to do that anymore, and when she kept on, then I just turned and started to leave. That was when she suddenly started screaming and pounding me on the chest. I can still see those fists of hers raining onto me, banging me as hard as she could, and I was so shocked and so scared I didn't know what to do at first. Finally I just grabbed her and tried to calm her down, but nothing worked. She could not accept that we were no longer lovers. She just kept screaming until she wore herself out.

"Marilyn," I finally said, "can't you see? It's over. It's been over for a long time now."

But she wouldn't listen to me, wouldn't believe me. Why, there were even a few times when she drove down to Long Beach to visit my parents. That November, too, she gave me a surprise thirty-fifth birthday party, and Larry, who was in on the surprise, drove me out. At the end of the evening, which went off well enough, Marilyn pulled me aside and said, "Why don't you appreciate me doing this for you?" I assured her that I did appreciate the gesture.

"So why are you going home with Larry, then?" she asked.

The situation was impossible now. Not long after the birthday party, still furious, she called me up to announce to me that she had taken all my clothes and thrown them out of the house—literally, out on the ground. I tried to be as calm as I could. "Marilyn, don't you understand that the house is Larry's and mine, and that you should be leaving the house, not my clothes?" I said. But to no avail. Another time, when I was visiting the house, she suddenly brought out a number of my letters, and she held them up and cried out, "This would make a great book!"

So by now it was apparent to me that Marilyn was growing even more unstable. And still, I wanted so to help her. I suggested that she see a psychologist, the same one that I had been to before. Marilyn followed my suggestion, at least for a while. Later I talked with the psychologist, and he recommended that I totally disconnect myself from her.

"That's the only way you can help Marilyn Barnett," the psychologist told me. "As long as you are in her life in any way, she will refuse to live her own life. You must take your suffering away as the final gift."

At last, Jim Jorgenson, my business manager, had a deal with Marilyn's lawyer. It was based on a telephone conversation I had had with Marilyn sometime late in 1979. Here is my testimony, when I was being examined by Marilyn's lawyer and he asked me about that call to her: "I just said, 'How does 50 percent of the net profits sound to you, if you have no further claims on my life, and if you will get out of the house, when the house is sold, keep paying rent until the house is sold, and do not be bothersome to me, but please give me the letters back, and have no further claims, no lawsuits, no publicity, nothing,' and she said that would be fine."

From there, the way it was worked out, a sum of $125,000 was agreed on as half the projected profit of the sale of the house. By April of 1981 I had advanced Marilyn $21,000 of the sum, and Jim Jorgenson then sent to Marilyn another check for $4,000, this time payable to her lawyer, with the understanding that Marilyn would vacate the house and give back the letters and honor the rest of our agreement. We would put up the remaining $100,000 in escrow, as they would the letters. But she wouldn't leave the house or give the letters back.

So Jim called Marilyn's lawyer again, and this is how he related that conversation at the trial:

"I told him the end of the month was coming around quickly, I hadn't seen any papers from him and I wanted to ask him the status of our agreement and he said that he had some bad news for me and my client.

"He said that the deal is off, that he had read the letters, that Marilyn had found more letters at the house and there were over a hundred letters instead of the 50 to 60 that he had originally procured from the safety deposit box and that Marilyn was entitled to a lot more than $125,000, that she was entitled to the house and a lot more. . . ."

When I heard that, my heart dropped. "They're going to hurt us," I told Larry and I told close friends—Dennis Wasser and Henry Holmes, our lawyers who were representing me and Larry in the litigation. "They are. They're really going to hurt us badly before this is over." Even before Marilyn sued, I sensed where she was taking matters. I felt that, like so much of my life, this, too, would ultimately be played out in public.

5 THE MOFFITTS OF LONG BEACH

In 1975 I planned to retire, and after I beat Chris in the semifinals at Wimbledon, I said, "I think I've been the most fortunate woman athlete who ever lived up to this time." I meant that. Whatever happens, I believe that, compared to everyone else, I've got the world by the tail. I was given more than most people. Then again, I also think I've used what I was given better than most people manage their talents. So, while I'm grateful, I don't feel guilty. I've earned it. Besides, I'm not surprised at all the success I've had. I mentioned that time when I was five or six and told my mother I'd be the best in something; by the time I was twelve, I knew what I'd be best in.

My pastor then was the Reverend Bob Richards, the Olympic gold medal–winning pole-vaulter and preacher, who was on all the Wheaties boxes. And one day I was with Reverend Bob, and he asked me, "Billie Jean, what are you going to do with your life?" You know the way ministers like to ask those kind of questions.

I think he thought I was going to say, "I want to devote my life to helping those less fortunate than I," something safe like that; but instead I shot back, "Reverend, I'm going to be the best tennis player in the world." Boy, I'll tell you, I still remember, that just about knocked his socks off.

But I was a very religious child growing up. Ours was a church household. Every day at school I participated in Youth for Christ and every night I read faithfully from the Bible. Besides, in those days, and especially if you were a girl, you weren't supposed to be too aggressive in anything, even your dreams. Obviously, by the time I laid my plans out to the Reverend Richards, I was leveling with myself, but in fact, just before that time I went through a period when I seriously expected to be a missionary.

In 1981, Chris and I were talking at the French Open one day, and she asked me if I had ever wanted to be anything especially when I was growing up, and I said, "Sure, I wanted to be a missionary."

And she started really laughing. I don't mean giggling. She was just beside herself. And I said, "Hey, it's not that funny. It's not impossible, you know."

And Chrissie said, "No, no, I'm not laughing at you. The reason I'm laughing is because I wanted to be a social worker." It was very funny.

Chris and I are really quite a lot alike in many ways, and certainly in the matter of our upbringing. Besides, if you were a little girl back then, back before I beat Bobby Riggs and slew the beast of male chauvinism, if you were a little girl who dared to aspire to a career at all, then it better not be one involved with a lot of money; maybe nurse or teacher—stewardess if you had some looks. Sometimes, even now, I don't think it's that women are more prominent that upsets some men—especially the older ones; it's just when we make a lot of money.

And to tell you the truth, I think I could have made a whale of a missionary (missionaress? missionette?). I've always been a leader. Even when I was a teenager—if I ever really was a teenager. I was so serious then; the other girl players would come to me for advice and counsel, even though I was the youngest in the group. I affect people. I know that. I don't know why, and I don't necessarily make an effort to, but I do. Larry, who sometimes has to define me for myself, told me once, "You have unbelievable power. You haven't asked for it, but you have it, and that's the way it is."

Whatever, I made myself what I am. My parents were devoted to me (and my brother), affectionate and enthusiastic, but they certainly never pushed me front and center. Besides, at the time I was growing up, who in their right mind would have pushed their daughter into tennis? There wasn't a nickel in it, and you were literally called a bum if you stayed in it long enough to be any good. Some reward.

Actually, even today, when the kids come in it so young, I don't know of a single one who really succeeded because a parent shoved her into the game, into tournaments. There was one player a few years ago who was a pretty fair prospect, but she really didn't like the game that much and she only stuck at it because her father made her. It was terrible. He would beat her if she lost. Not surprisingly, she never developed past a certain level, and all she really wanted to do was get out of the game. Even when she was a player, she would hang around with the press as much as possible, instead of the other players. It wasn't that she didn't like us; it was just that she associated us with the pain of having to play. And first thing she did when she got old enough was to cut and run altogether.

Julie Heldman was another example. She certainly wasn't pushed into the sport—she was much too smart to allow that—but her father had been a fine player, and her mother, Gladys, had not only become a top player herself but, with *World Tennis* magazine, she had become a real power in the game. So, in Julie's case, I think she felt family pressure to succeed, but also it came from within. She was so brittle that her determination to become number one—and the frustration that she couldn't—would literally make her sick. Yet as different as Julie and I were in many ways, she would come to me for heart-to-hearts. I remember one time particularly, at The Queen's Club in London, where we sat together on those little benches there and she spilled out to me how agonizing it all was.

"Julie," I said, "then *don't play*. You don't have to be number one or number ten. You don't have to play at all. Just do what makes you happy." None of that was especially original or trenchant philosophy, but it was obviously a relief for her to hear that from somebody like me who had done better than she in the game.

People made a big to-do about Chris when she came on at such a young age, and then, after her, the ones even younger: Tracy Austin, Pam Shriver, Andrea Jaeger, Kathy Horvath, Kathy Rinaldi. In many of these cases the girls had a father who played a prominent role in encouraging them and directing them. But what is even more obvious in all the cases is that the girls just loved the game. Their fathers would have had to beat them to make them stay away from the courts. Past a certain point, no matter how much a parent may want a daughter to be a champion, there is just nothing they can do. The girl has to want it and do it for herself.

What you do need from your parents if you are going to succeed is their willingness to sacrifice for you. People are always asking why there aren't more good black players in the game. I was talking once to Roland Jaeger, Andrea's father, and he pointed out to me that the black girls who have begun to have some success in tennis are all from fairly comfortable, middle-class backgrounds. Renee Blount's father is a surgeon; Leslie Allen's mother is a Broadway actress; Diane Morrison's father is an engineer, her mother a psychol-

ogist; the late Andrea Buchanan's parents are both techni-
cians. Leslie Allen and her mother live in a town house in
Harlem, and whenever she comes out on the streets in her
warm-up suit, the kids there go, "You in track, sister? You in
basketball?" It would never occur to them to think of *tennis*.

So you see, it isn't blacks that tennis lacks; it is a lack of
economically poor girls—of whatever race. If a girl is going to
make it as a young player—and if you don't make it when
you're very young, you seem to be out of luck—then she needs
one or both of her parents driving her around, buying equip-
ment, and generally devoting an awful lot of time to their
daughter's quest. And obviously, poorer families simply can't
manage that on a child's behalf.

People are always trying to get me to visit some low-income
area of a city and give a clinic or something, but for a long
time now I have absolutely refused to do this unless I could be
shown that there is an ongoing sports program in that community. Otherwise, it's just an ego trip for the athlete, making
the public think how wonderful he or she is to help the poor
children. But in fact, all you may be doing is teasing them
without offering them any real chance. It's not unlike me
going to that professional baseball game when I was nine.
From what I understand from my black friends, the National
Junior Tennis League, which takes tennis into the ghettos,
gets the youngsters interested in tennis but does not then
offer a good sustaining program. But then, maybe no organization in an individual sport can bring the best players along
so well as the parents who have time and money.

This is all especially depressing to me because one of the
great dreams of my life is to see tennis become a game for all
people, and not just for the wealthy. Obviously, great strides
have been made in this direction in the last generation, but it
is still apparent that the poorer you are, the less chance you
have of making it in tennis—and, conversely, the better
chance in some team sport, where coaching and competition

are less a function of the family pocketbook. This is one reason why Team Tennis is so important to Larry and me.

To me, the most wonderful thing about Team Tennis is not only that it is one of those rare athletic events that involve both genders, but that it also features every possible game of tennis—men's and women's singles, men's and women's doubles, and mixed doubles. Plus, there is variety in the order of play, too, as the captains can decide how to schedule the matches. I only wish that all tennis could be settled as decisively as our team game, too. We have no ad points. At 40-all, the next point decides the game. And if a set goes to 6-all, the tiebreaker is the nine-point sudden death, not the twelve-point lingering death. To me, there is nothing more exciting in tennis—in sports—than when a set in Team Tennis is tied at 6 and the tiebreaker is tied at 4, and the decision rests on one point. Of course the pressure is excruciating, but every athlete, in every sport, should have to face that now-or-never moment at some point. Tennis gives too many second chances.

Anyway, in my own case, when I was growing up and we were struggling middle-class, I had to depend on my parents to make the difference. No matter how talented I might have been, how could I have improved if my mother hadn't driven me all over Southern California so I could play the best players? There is a certain irony in that, too, because I wouldn't have had the same advantages in the advanced 1980s, if I were growing up now, as I had in the medieval 1950s. You see, then it was not uncommon for the mother to be a full-time housewife. Now, you can be sure, my mother would also be working outside the house—at least part-time—and she wouldn't have the time to help me be a player. A lot of the best players I grew up with came from fairly modest households. Like me, they probably wouldn't be able to compete with the richer kids today because neither of their parents would be able to help them day to day.

When I was growing up—and certainly at the Moffitts' in Long Beach—there were more defined roles. In my house, too, Dad made the money and Mom ran the home. But I'll say this because it made an impression on me: the two of them shared a lot of the work around the house; I grew up with a good sense of teamwork between a man and a woman. And to help Randy and me be able to play sports, Mom did pick up a little money on the side, too, selling Avon products or holding Tupperware parties. Boy, were we typical: Exhibit A, American Dream, Southern California Division. There was one boy, one girl—one of each. Randy was five years younger than I. And at home everybody actually called me "Sis." I mean, it was like *The Life of Riley,* straight out of TV.

My mother was the change of pace in the house. She was the peacemaker and the most refined one, and when it was called for, she could put us all in our place by playing the long-suffering martyr. My father adored all sports—playing them, watching them, listening to them, talking about them—and I would have to say that Mom got kind of gypped because not only did her son end up being involved in sports—Randy pitched nine seasons for the San Francisco Giants—but so did her daughter. Even when I grew so devoted to tennis, she made me stay with my piano lessons.

I was always a tomboy. It was probably appropriate that I was named for my father. I was going to be called Michelle Louise if I was a girl (MICHELLE LOUISE WHIPS BOBBY RIGGS IN STRAIGHT SETS—does that sound any better?), but my father had been called off to the war when I was born, so my mother decided she better not take any chances, and so she named me after him. He's Bill; Mom is Betty. Bill and Betty, Randy and Sis.

My father is hardly some macho crazy frustrated athlete, though. As I said, he worked with Mom. My first memories of him are of my waking up to hear him down in the kitchen making coffee, listening to the big-band music on the radio.

Firemen work twenty-four hours on, twenty-four off, so every other day he would come home first thing in the morning and start the breakfast while Mom was still sleeping. He loved music, too. Just like Mom. They still adore those big bands. They used to dance to them in the house. They've always been terrific ballroom dancers. If ever they could afford to go out together, it would be dancing.

Dad was a very affectionate father, too. Every night, he would make us all kiss each other goodnight, no matter what, because he always said that you never could tell when something might happen, and if it did, and if one of us never saw the others again, it would be terrible if we had forgotten to kiss the rest of the family goodnight.

In fact, of all the incorrect criticism I've received, the one thing that always hurt me the most was the business about me hating men. I've spent my whole life snuggling up to Dad or Larry, one or the other. I'm still such a little baby girl when I'm around Dad. I just climb onto his lap and cuddle up. I'll never stop loving being a baby for my father.

Of course, this isn't to say that Dad and I haven't had our conflicts, too. So much of my competitive spirit (good) and temper (bad) comes from Daddy. He was still playing recreational basketball back when I was starting out in tennis, and all his lectures to me about being a good sport and not arguing on the courts were undercut because every time I went to see him play he was the absolute worst, screaming and cursing and stomping around; do as I say, not as I do. But Dad could put his foot down, too. Once, when he thought I had simply gone too far with bad behavior on the court, he told me that if I ever did anything like that again, he was taking my racket away. Then, to drive the point home, he took the racket out to the garage and starting running the power saw. I really thought he was going to saw my racket in half. I straightened out fast.

And if I still sit on Daddy's lap and coo at him, we can still go at it, too. In the summer of 1981, he came to one of my Team Tennis matches at the Forum in Los Angeles. Now, this was not long after the Marilyn suit was revealed, one of the first times I was back on the courts in public. I was uptight and self-conscious. And just before we were about to start the match, when our whole team was huddled together, clasping hands and all that, my father appears out of nowhere and he leans right in with a program for me to autograph. He had struck up a conversation with some kid in the stands, and the boy said he was a fan of mine, and my father had said, "Sure, I can get you Billie Jean's autograph," and so he marched right down to the team bench to do it.

I was burned up. Would he pop into the bullpen when Randy was warming up in the seventh inning to ask for an autograph for some little Giant fan? Of course not. So I turned on Dad, and cold as ice, I said, "Who do you think you are?"—you know: How can you come in here, bugging me like this? And that really infuriated him—besides making him look like a loser to the little boy. He was so angry that when he turned around and saw Larry, he said, "That's for her!" And flipped the finger. My father! For me! His darling daughter!

Well, Larry was on me for the next few days to please call my father and patch things back up, and finally I did—I let him simmer for a few days (and I needed the time to cool down myself)—and Dad came to the phone when Mom called him, and even before I could say a word, here he is, almost in baby talk, gurgling into the receiver, "And how's my little baby girl?"

I mean, it just broke me up.

If there are any problems with my father and me, it is that we've always understood each other too well.

His family moved to Southern California when he was thirteen, from Montana. My mother's family had come out earlier. I couldn't begin to tell you my genealogy in any detail, except I know it is English and Scotch-Irish, mostly. It is hard to trace anything with my family because both my grandparents on my Dad's side had been adopted and took new names. I do know this, though, that we are so completely All-American that I even have Indian blood in me. My mother's grandfather married a Seminole squaw. I love the way Indians look, too, but I didn't seem to get any of that except the stubby legs.

I didn't have a weight problem originally. I was just one of those people who became fat overnight. It was the first summer I ever traveled East—in 1959, when I was fifteen—and we spent a lot of time in Philadelphia, and they had the best ice cream there. In fact, I've never forgotten the two brand names that I gorged myself on: Bassett's and Dolly Madison. I was five feet four, and I gained twenty-five pounds in less than a month, which is quite a feat, especially since I was exercising the whole time. One night at two o'clock, the other players I was traveling with, Karen Hantze, Kathy Chabot, Carole Caldwell, Barbara Browning, and Pam Davis, woke me up out of a dead sleep and gave me a haircut. They were just having fun, and I'm never very alert when I first wake up, especially at two in the morning, and so I just sort of lent them my head for a while and then went back to sleep.

The haircut they gave me was a squarer, shorter version of what I had been wearing, and that made me look even fatter than I was from the ice cream. I was so blown up that by the time it came to fly back to California, I could only jam myself into one dress, a bright pink one. I looked something like a powder puff, and honest to God, when I got off the plane, I was such a different creature from what had left that both my parents walked right past me, looking for Billie Jean.

But I wasn't really bothered all that much. I never hated my body or was ashamed of it. I always had a boyfriend. I was getting along well in school and in church, and the extra weight didn't seem to affect my tennis game. I was just plain fat and happy. Remember, too, that the things written about me always exaggerated the Moffitts' financial straits. We weren't nearly as poor as it was fashionable to make us out to be. It was just that anybody in tennis who wasn't in the country club was always stereotyped as indigent. Pancho Gonzales was the classic case of this misrepresentation. Certainly, he did suffer some racial discrimination, but he was hardly the ghetto immigrant that most people assumed from the press; instead, like me, he came from a stable middle-class Southern California family with a strong father and an adoring mother.

We lived in a neat tract house in a nice neighborhood. We had three bedrooms for my parents, Randy, and me; the bad news is that we only had one bathroom. My father built a garage for the house himself, and when I won an extra radio in a tennis tournament in 1957—one of my first superduper prizes—I gave it to my father, and he took it out to the garage, and it's still there. I think that's where most of my trophies are, too, although I've sort of lost track of them. I was never very big on displaying trays and trophies and all those things. I would just bring them home and give them to Mom and Dad and forget about it after that. I *guess* they're all out in the garage with the radio.

I did have my own bedroom, even if that's about what it was—room for a bed. But I certainly never felt deprived in any way, although especially as I got into tennis and encountered people who lived with so much more, I understood better how many things there were that we could not manage. It never ate at me. Besides, there had always been a lot of pretty rich kids where I went to school—at Polytechnic High, in Long Beach.

In fact, that probably gave me a lot of incentive, if only subconsciously. It isn't, after all, just the very poorest kids who are so determined to scratch their way up the ladder. It's social and financial relativity that's so important to a little girl or boy. If a child is terribly poor, but so is everybody else around in that small world, then the child's own personal deprivation may not make that much of an imprint. But being a little bit less advantaged in a middle-class world gave me a great drive. I read somewhere once that Jack Nicklaus's family belonged to a country club when he was growing up, but his father was a druggist and in the country-club pecking order that wasn't much, so that drove Nicklaus to work harder to excel at golf than the other, relatively more privileged boys. Maybe that's the best of all worlds that you could have, growing up: poorest kid in the country club.

We had to save change for my first tennis racket—eight dollars' worth of pennies and nickels and a few dimes in a mason jar that we took down to Brown's Sporting Goods. What kind of racket did I buy? An eight-dollar kind. It had a lavender-colored throat; it had lavender strings. Not many of those around. And it was the one and only tennis racket I ever had to buy, because once you show any promise at all, a racket company will pop in and start supplying you freebies from the company store.

The single occasion where finances really hurt me was the summer of 1958, when I was fourteen and being recognized as a real prospect for the first time, one of the best fifteen-and-under players around. Perry Jones, who ran the Southern California Tennis Association, decreed that I could go to the national championships, which were being held in Middletown, Ohio—*if* I beat Kathy Chabot, who I had never beaten before. He didn't think I had a prayer. But the opportunity so excited me that I started getting up at five-thirty in the morning so I could jump rope and do other exercises, and I worked out that way for two months, and I not only beat Kathy, I beat her in straight sets, three and four, and I beat her at her own game, from the backcourt. I could play that way when I set my mind to it, even though I was instinctively an attacking player from the first day I hit a ball. One time, though, I played a baseline game with Barbara Browning, and I rallied with her for four and a half hours before I won. I couldn't even get out of bed the next day.

But anyway, since I beat Kathy, Mr. Jones had to let me go to Ohio for the nationals. In those days, before open tennis, the amateur pooh-bahs, like Mr. Jones (everybody always called him *Mr.*, and I can't stop myself from doing it even now, no matter how much I disliked that man), could make or break you. Mr. Jones had even more power because, at least until about this time, Southern California produced a preponderance of the best players in the country. He was a fussy old bachelor who hated girls. The boys got all the breaks in the Association. Of course, it helped to have money, too. If you did, the parents could donate some and get a tax write-off, and then Mr. Jones would use the money to send the rich parents' kid off to the tournament. It was a public-service laundering.

Obviously, the Moffitts of Long Beach were not up to that, but I had established such a record that Mr. Jones simply could not deny me the trip to Middletown. It wasn't going to cost him a nickel, either, because the Long Beach Tennis Patrons and the Long Beach Century Club staked me to $350. That was more than enough to cover air fare and reasonable living expenses. But then, to completely dampen my euphoria, Mr. Jones declared that I was too young and, as a girl, would require a chaperon. This was absolute discrimination. The players stayed with families, and I certainly was old enough to be put on a plane and met at the other end. But Mr. Jones would not listen.

So finally we decided that if my mother and I traveled by railroad, the two of us could manage. We sat up in the coach for three nights to get to Middletown, and we lived as frugally as was possible. When we got there, it was the first time I had ever played on clay, and I was beaten in the quarterfinals by Carol Hanks of St. Louis, even though I was seeded number four. But I really wasn't discouraged. I knew the strange new surface had made it difficult for me, and—more important—I had seen the competition from all over the country and I was not at all intimidated by what I had seen.

Also, I had a wonderful time.

And then the tournament was over and it was time for Mom and me to get on the train and go back to California. Many of the other girls were getting in cars to go to the airport—but not to fly back home. Instead, they were all going on to Philadelphia, where the next tournament was being held. That broke my heart. A lot of the ones going East weren't nearly as good as I was.

I can remember so vividly standing on the corner with my mother and just fighting back the tears as I said good-bye to the other players. As soon as they were all gone, I turned to Mom and I said, "This is never going to happen to me again."

She felt as badly about things as I did. She said, "Don't worry, Billie Jean. If we can get the money, we—"

"Oh, no, no," I cried out. "Either I'll be good enough and get them to pay the money for me or I don't want to come."

When Dad and Randy met us back at Union Station in L.A., Mom and I had something like a dollar left between us.

6 SAVED FROM BUMDOM

When I was fifteen I had an assignment in school to write a theme, and I chose to detail what I hoped and imagined my future would hold. The story began with my first trip to Wimbledon, which I guessed would be three years later, in 1962 (actually, I was to make it the year before, 1961). "Thump, thump, thump, beat my heart," I began. "This can't be true. Here I am in New York City at 5 p.m. leaving by plane for Wimbledon, England. I still can't believe it. Here I am, 18 years of age, and in one week I will be participating in what is considered to be the Tennis Championships of the World."

And my tale goes on. Aboard the plane I chance to meet Ramsey Earnhart, who was then one of the brightest—and cutest—tennis prospects in Southern California. He went on to play at the University of Southern California, on the great teams headed by Rafael Osuna and Dennis Ralston. I had a crush on Ramsey. And then, in London, I am greeted by Darlene Hard, who was then the top player in the United States. Darlene, as I had it, had shipped her car to London for the tournament so she could tool all around between matches. It was, I carefully reported, "a red '50 Chevy convertible, slightly lowered, with twin pipes." And it was Darlene, in my saga, who eventually eliminated me, although I carried her to 10–8 in the third in the quarterfinals. And with that magnificent match ended my first fantasy trip to Wimbledon.

But I added a short epilogue, which was to take place in 1988, when I would be forty-five years old, and it tells more about me and my mind at that time than all I wrote before. It goes: "Here I am at home 27 years later, sitting with my four wonderful children (at times they're wonderful). After the summer of '61 I entered Pomona College, in California, spending five years and graduating with a Masters Degree. I married Ramsey Earnhart—remember that boy I met on the way to the plane that day? Even though I never did achieve my ambition in tennis, I'm so glad I went ahead and received a higher education than high school, instead of turning out to be a tennis bum."

Of course, as you may know, none of that quite happened, and despite all my best adolescent intentions. I have to thank Larry for that. I married him so I could be an honest woman, and then he was the one person who gave me the courage to go back to being a bum.

As I told my mother, as I told Bob Richards, I always wanted to be special, to be the best in one thing. I've always thought it would have been easier for me just to be comfortable, to have found a fireman of my own and had two children, but I really had no choice. I was driven. All people who succeed must have some sense of destiny, because anyone needs a measure of that spirit to offset the prevailing attitudes around them—or, at least, the ones that existed during the fifties. Especially if you were a middle-class

WASP, as I was, the great pressure on you was to be well rounded. Yes, the American Dream was still in place, but you were only supposed to succeed by being pretty good at a lot of things, rather than by being very good at one thing. Don't put yourself on the line. Don't risk it.

The British, for best example, are still like that—in spades. They don't like winners at all. I don't mean they like losers. Not exactly. What the British like is r/u's—runner-ups. Almost. I hate r/u's. I don't see any sense in that at all. In fact, that is what sets a lot of us champions apart. John Newcombe, who had as much in the way of guts as anybody who ever played any sport, tells the story about the time he and Angie were having a big party back in Australia. There was a silver dish full of chicken, and when the guests ate their way to the bottom, they saw that the plate had an inscription on it. "What the hell is this, mate?" they asked Newcombe.

He showed them the writing. "See, I got this for being runner-up in 1966 to Stolle at Forest Hills," he said. And his friends hooted at Newc and screamed at him derisively for displaying any sort of tribute to being a runner-up, and then, according to Newcombe, they took the silver plate outside, urinated all over it, and left it there, in the bushes. And some people still ask me why the Aussies used to win so much. They just didn't tolerate r/u's, even when it was John Newcombe.

But at the time I met Larry, I was quite happy to settle in with a normal life that would permit me to be a happy r/u.

We were introduced in the library at L.A. State, which we were both attending. I had been told that this Larry King was a really handsome guy, and my first thought was, Yeah, he really *is* handsome. Larry liked the way I looked, too. He still remembers clearly that he liked my eyes and my rear end best, although not necessarily in that order. I had on a corduroy wraparound skirt. He says. I don't remember. He does. It was love at first sight.

At the time, Larry was studying to be a biochemist, which

made sense because he is a terribly analytical person. As much as he loved biochemistry, though, he likes moving around, being involved with lots of people. "I just can't stand being all cooped up in that laboratory," he said. So I told him, Well, don't. Do something else. We talked it over and he decided to be a lawyer. Whatever Larry might technically be defined as, what he really does is solve problems. That they might be in a laboratory or in tennis or in business—wherever—is all rather incidental. For example, not long ago, Larry invented an ashtray. It sucked the smoke down into it, which was fantastic because people could go right on smoking if they absolutely had to, but without having the smoke louse up the air and bother anyone else's lungs. (Unfortunately, it was not a great idea if you were selling it, we discovered. Nonsmokers don't buy ashtrays, and smokers don't care where their smoke goes.) But anyway, the invention tells a lot about Larry.

But if I encouraged Larry to switch over to law, his influence on me was even greater. He was the one who pointed out to me how ludicrously unfair it was that I wasn't receiving an athletic scholarship. Tuition was only forty-seven dollars a semester at L.A. State, but even though I was the best player on campus and one of the best female players in the world and easily the best-known athlete at the college, I didn't get a nickel's worth of assistance. By contrast, Larry, who is a good club player, but no more than that, was getting a full scholarship—as the seventh man on a six-man team. We forget now, but it's only been in the last decade that women started getting athletic scholarships.

It was not that this sort of double standard had never entered my mind before, even though it was right there at home for me to see. For example, I was always advised that if we didn't have enough money for both of us children to attend college, then Randy would be the one to go. And even though I was always more responsible than Randy, he could ride his bicycle all over the place but I wasn't allowed to enjoy anything like his privileges. "Why?" I asked. "Because you're a girl," my father said. Still, even if that sort of thing upset me and seemed unfair—*un-American*—I accepted it. It was just the way things were, always had been, and always would be.

And when we got married, the way things were, I would give up whatever I was interested in and stay at home and take care of the house and the babies I would have. And Larry would work. At first, though, I helped put him through law school with what I could scrounge out of the shamateur game. In fact, Larry told me afterward that he owed me one, that if I ever wanted to get a law degree for myself, he'd support me through that.

"But I don't want to be a lawyer," I said.

"Yeah, I know you don't," he said. "But people listen to you more if you've passed the bar. It's ridiculous, of course, but that's the way it is."

Where Larry *supported* me—why he really doesn't owe me one—is the way he encouraged me to go for it all. Once I had achieved a certain high status in the game, a top-ten ranking and all that, I was really quite satisfied. From the time I was seventeen, for the next four years or so, I really drifted. It was fun, and maybe I would even win something. Or maybe not. But mainly I was just marking time until Larry and I could get married and start a real life. And he couldn't understand me. "Billie Jean," he said, "I just don't see how you can give up something where you have the potential to be best in the world—the best of all."

He made me think about things differently and become more curious and more challenged. Then, in the winter of 1964, during my senior year at L.A. State, an Australian businessman named Bob Mitchell offered me a chance to go to Australia and train with Mervyn Rose, who was a very accomplished coach. Rose had been a world-class player, too,

an Aussie Davis Cup player, second string to Frank Sedgman.
But I hesitated about accepting the offer. And then Larry said,
"Go, Billie Jean. Don't worry. I'll be here when you get back."

And so I left college and my fiancé. Larry took nineteen
units and worked in a factory so he could afford to call me all
the time. Rose revamped large parts of my game. He made
me junk my American twist serve, teaching me a slice instead, and he redid my forehand, which has always been my
weaker side. In fact, in many respects it was like starting all
over again. Soon, although I was ranked in the top five in the
world, I was having trouble beating run-of-the-mill Aussie
players in minor state championships. I could have regularly
used the great line Rafe Osuna got off once when he lost to a
semiretired Ham Richardson. "They tell me Ham is a weekend player," Osuna said, "and just my luck, I play him on the
weekend."

The problem was that Rose couldn't just tinker with my
game. He had to take me several steps back before I could go
forward. Don Budge made the same sort of drastic revisions
with his forehand one winter when he was number three in
the world. For a while, he couldn't beat anybody. Bill Tilden
had to relearn his whole backhand when he was number two.
But that's what you have to do if you don't want to remain as
an r/u.

Worse, I told everybody why I was going to Australia: *I'm
shooting to be number one.* It scared me to put myself on the
line like that, but I understood that if I declared my honest
intentions in the open, it would drive me all the more. People
are always asking me what makes a champion. Well, in many
respects the simplest definition is: a champion is the one with
self-awareness who is closest to reality and seems to be able
to execute best under pressure.

It took a long time, too, before everything began to fall into
place, but that next September, 1965, I made the finals at
Forest Hills for the first time. I was playing Margaret, and I
had her 5–3 in both sets, and I lost both of them, playing

stupidly. I looked foolish, too. I was marrying Larry in four days, and I had a new permanent for the occasion. And then the people who ran the USLTA forgot to give me my trophy. Bobby Kennedy, who was a U.S. senator then, was making the presentations, and someone had to sort of drag him back when it at last dawned on one of the big muckety-mucks that there had also been a stubby little American girl on the court with the champion.

I was devastated that I lost. Afterward, Frank Brennan, who was helping to coach me at the time, reminded me how Margaret had lobbed me well over my left shoulder. I would reach back and hit high backhand volleys in return. Mr. Brennan pointed out that, had I hustled just a bit more, I could have taken an extra step to my left, run back and around several of those lobs, and slammed them back at Margaret. Just that little extra effort could have been enough. His analysis depressed me even more, so we decided to go to a movie, which happened to be *The Pawnbroker*, which is even more depressing. It was a terrible day.

(By the way, let me say this here. You will notice that invariably I talk about "Margaret," as I have in this section, or "Chris" or "Martina" or "Tracy" and so on, but in the next paragraph I will be referring to "McEnroe" and "Borg" and "Connors," etc. I know that's not proper or fair or equal. But it's just the way it is. People say, "McEnroe will be playing Borg, and Chrissie will be playing Hana." Maybe someday soon we won't be saying that, but we do now, and so for natural purposes of clarity, I'm just following the line of least resistance.)

Anyway, the loss to Margaret at least showed me that my trip to Australia had paid off, that I was in her class and could beat her soon enough. And, comforted by that, I went back to California and got married and settled in. Larry was still an undergraduate, and we didn't have any money. Our idea of heaven was to scrimp and save all week so that on Saturday night we could go out to a franchise place called Winchell's and splurge on a doughnut and then go to a movie. A few months later I came into some real big money because I was given eight dollars an hour for teaching kids to play out at a place called Foothills—four hours every weekend, thirty-two bucks. Of course, that was against all the amateur rules and could have disqualified me for life, but it was all a fraud—everybody in the whole sport cheated some.

The honeymoon ended when I went out on the tour again that summer—and Larry came with me. I won my first Wimbledon and just about lost a husband. Larry just couldn't tolerate hanging around like a puppy dog. A lot of tennis husbands rather enjoy it, but Larry was plain going crazy. He was absolutely wonderful, too. I was sick for virtually all of the summer with diarrhea, which was subsequently diagnosed as colitis; then I hardly got out of bed all winter.

But the summer was a slow death for him. Right after Wimbledon we had to drive to Wales, where I was committed to play, but I was horribly sick even before I got there. But I played. I always played. That's what you did in those days. By the time Larry and I reached the national doubles championships the next month in Brookline, Massachusetts, I had combat fatigue; and one day, in the house where we were staying as guests, I came apart at the seams, and I started beating on Larry and screaming at him, "You don't care! You don't care! You don't care!"

And, of course, he had already been with me for weeks, literally caring for me the whole summer.

We were smart enough never to try that again.

It doesn't work any better when the shoe is on the other foot, either. I can't stand to hang out with Larry when he is promoting one of his tournaments. The phone is ringing constantly; he is distracted, going full out, totally involved in business—and all it would do is louse me up so that I couldn't play well. As a consequence, after we understood the situation, if I came to play in a tournament that Larry was promoting, then I would take another room. Would you sleep in your husband's office? But, of course, everybody thought that was really curious, and proof that the Kings didn't have a real, normal marriage.

Of course, for a female athlete there's almost no way you can win, because there is such an inordinate amount of attention paid to our personal lives. The press is much more knowledgeable and professional now, but it was not so long ago when this was a typical press conference after a 5–7, 6–4, 7–6 final:

"Billie Jean, did Larry see the match?"

"Are you planning to have children soon?"

"Chris, have you spoken to Jimmy recently?"

"Did someone special give you that necklace?"

"Billie Jean, how is your marriage?"

"How often do you and Larry see each other?"

"Is it hard combining marriage and a career?"

"Chris, when did you change your hair?"

"Oh, by the way, what was the turning point in the match?"

One thing Larry and I never had a problem with was that it never bothered him that I was getting all the attention. In fact, I don't think any spouse could ever have accepted that situation as well as Larry. Often, when people would come up to him for an autograph, he would sign it "Mr. Billie Jean King." That would upset me, but he would just laugh and say, "Oh, come on. Those people only know me through you. It's right this way." Larry's amazing that way. Nothing ever seems to bother him.

That drives me crazy. It's like living with the Tar Baby— and all the worse, because I'm so mercurial. Most of our arguments are about the same thing. For that matter, most of our arguments even sound identical. One of two related things invariably trigger them:

1. After a long time of being apart, we are at last together again, and he says we are going out with So-and-So to Such-and-Such, and I say, I don't want to, I want to be with you,

and he says, But you will be with me, and I say, No, not if we go out, because then I'm on display, and sure, you can still be you, but I can't be me, and why can't we be alone? And on and on, like that.

The funny thing is, Larry loves big groups and hates the spotlight, while I'm a ham who prefers it intimate.

Or:

2. Larry says, Billie Jean, you consume me. You demand total, absolute attention, and not only that but you demand it on your own terms, and so even when I am trying to give you total, absolute attention, you start talking to the waiter. And then I scream, Yes, and you want to know why? Because the waiter at least gives more than you, and in ten minutes I know more about him than I know about you after twenty years.

Larry is glad when he hears me get to that part, because he knows so well from past experience that that is my best shot, and that after that part of the routine I will almost surely turn sweet and loving.

Unquestionably, we do find it hard to communicate emotionally. Opposites attract and all that, I guess. Larry's mother died when he was two, and I know he lost something there that he can never obtain somewhere else. Sometimes I think that the simplest way to describe the differences in us is to say that there's a lot of baby talk in me but there's none in Larry.

We are so different in so many ways that divorce has pretty much been a constant possibility since 1969 or so, four or five years after we were married. Things just accumulated. The only problem is that we are so much in love with each other. That is what would complicate any divorce.

Of course, I understand how hard it is for most people to appreciate the sort of marriage that we do have. It doesn't fit into any sort of neat niche, and that irritates a lot of people. Long before the Marilyn affair came out, I had the distinct feeling that many people were not just uncommonly curious about our marriage, but that they really were rooting against it. I always felt a prevailing sense of disappointment every time I declared that it looked like the Kings' marriage was going to head into another week.

Marriage is difficult and tenuous enough, even under what are supposed to be ideal circumstances, and so I suppose many of the critical people have been angry at me because I shouldn't have the right to have such an atypical marriage still lasting. Besides—and always—any marriage where the woman is more of the breadwinner is going to come under even more suspicious scrutiny.

It also follows, for most people, that any man who would marry a rich and prominent athlete must be a wimpy guy. In fact, though, the reverse is more liable to be true. A young man who can stand up to that judgment, who can accept a different role, is liable, instead, to be a very strong, secure person. That not only applies to Larry but to most of the husbands of tennis players that I know.

Otherwise, the men and the marriages in women's tennis are as different as you would expect in any cross section. They fail, where they do, for all the usual reasons. I know one that broke up because the simple strains of traveling, of being apart, were too much. I know another that was a plain old case of basic sexual incompatibility. Jealousy did in another. He wasn't a player, and he became convinced that she was sleeping with one of her male teammates in World Team Tennis. Another one collapsed because the husband was a great chaser (and that wasn't just her imagination). Tennis marriages break up for exactly the same reasons as the marriages at your office do.

The marriages that do work are just as varied. If not mine and Larry's, then what could be more unusual than the Joneses, Pip and Ann? He is something like thirty-five years her senior, but they appear more compatible than anyone around us. I remember after Ann first met him, and everybody was trying to tell her that she was crazy to be mooning after this old guy, and she said to me, "So many people try to keep us apart just because he's older, but nobody ever asks me if I love Pip—and I do."

When Rosie Casals and Frankie Durr and I traveled with Ann as part of what was known as the National Tennis League in the late sixties, Pip came with Ann—and here he was, scuffling along the back roads of the world with a silly bunch of kid tennis players. And he was great. I remember one time we were stranded for a couple extra days in Sydney because some playing dates elsewhere had fallen through, and so we were just hanging around the hotel, time really dragging—and I was a special treat then, going through my Hermann Hesse period—and finally somebody took out a guitar and we started to sing, and Pip pitched in louder than anyone else. Now there was a husband!

But there's all kinds. Take a guy like Roger Cawley, who was a good English junior, who knows tennis, and who is even perfect for warming Evonne up, who is exactly her style and temperament. And then you take someone like Barry Court, who, as opposed to Margaret, came from a very wealthy background and, on top of that, had never played tennis seriously before he met her. And both of those marriages have worked wonderfully.

For one thing, remember that it isn't exactly difficult for a husband to troop the world with a woman who makes hundreds of thousands of dollars a year. And the ones with children have nannies, remember. It isn't exactly as if guys like Roger or Barry became typical househusbands, washing the bathroom floors every week and comparing detergents and whiteners all day long. It isn't a bad life, especially if the breadwinner is winning big.

And then, too, more and more you find players marrying each other—Chris Evert and John Lloyd, Bjorn Borg and

Mariana Simionescu, Raz Reid and Kerry Melville, Phil Dent and Bettyann Stuart—even if for most of the year the men's and women's tours are continents apart. But it doesn't take much; after all, players share a lot in common. That used to scare hell out of the USLTA.

When I was growing up in tennis, in the fifties, the officials were constantly telling us girl players, Whatever you do, don't marry a boy player. I didn't know it at the time, but they were also telling the boys, Whatever you do, don't marry a girl player. As far as I can remember, we never asked specifically why, and they never bothered to volunteer details. Knowing the USLTA, though, it probably wasn't marriage that worried its officials; it would be that a girl player and a boy player would be playing together nights without USLTA sanction.

Since the USLTA didn't govern tennis very well, it should come as no great shock to learn that it didn't manage very well intruding in the area of romance or sex, either. It did its damnedest to break up Karen Hantze and Rod Susman when they started going together. Karen was also from Southern California, my very good friend, and we surprised everybody in the world when we won the Wimbledon doubles, unseeded, my first year over there, 1961. Shortly after that we came back to the States and roomed together for the Wightman Cup matches in Chicago. Rod was nearby and I covered for Karen all the time. She would set the alarm and sneak off to see Rod at four o'clock in the morning. It couldn't have affected Karen too much the wrong way, either, inasmuch as she won both her singles and the doubles she played with me.

She married Rod, and the next year, too, she won Wimbledon, but shortly after that she dropped out of tennis. Rod was just a journeyman player, and he couldn't stay in the game, and it left him insanely jealous thinking of Karen off somewhere by herself on the circuit. So she quit for him and started raising a family. Karen did, in fact, pretty much what

I had always figured I would do. And years later, when tennis had boomed and Shelley, her daughter, was old enough, Karen came back and started playing in some tournaments, but she wouldn't stay on tour long enough, week after week, to get her effectiveness back. Today, I don't think a Rod Susman would ask that his wife stop playing, but then it is not fair to single him out for criticism of something that was typical thinking for that time. And I don't mean just toward women, either. Chuck McKinley was at the very height of his powers—a recent Wimbledon champion, like Karen—when his wife, Wylita, convinced him to give up the game. Karen became a housewife; Chuck became a stockbroker. Same thing, really. Whatever, you were not a tennis bum.

But if there was no future in tennis at that time, we were positive there must be one in marriage. There were five junior players, all from Southern California, that I was especially close to because of our common geography and because we all made the Junior Wightman Cup Team together: Karen, Carole Caldwell, Kathy Chabot, Barbara Browning, and Pam Davis. By the time I finally married Larry, at the advanced age of twenty-one, all the others were already wives. Twenty-one, and I was an old maid.

And, the wise admonitions of the USLTA notwithstanding, three of the six married tennis players. The top celebrity marriage was Carole to Clark Graebner, because both bride and groom became world class, and, in fact, both lost in the finals at Forest Hills (if in different years). Naturally, that is the marriage we all thought was the ideal one: Carole and Clark. And that is the only one of the six that didn't last.

Considering our ages, that is a pretty good batting average, too. Now, of course, there is so much less pressure for young people to get married so soon. In those days, it didn't matter: you could be a Wimbledon champion, Phi Beta Kappa, Miss America, Nobel Peace Prize winner, but if they asked you about marriage and you didn't at least have a hot prospect ready to get down on one knee, you knew you were considered to be no more than half a woman. Now, everybody can get married later and the urgency is gone. I was sitting in a press conference in 1981 when (naturally) someone asked Hana Mandlikova about her marriage plans. "I just want to be number one right now," she answered. "Maybe I will begin to think about marriage later."

So things are surely changing in that regard, and maybe that means that someday people will accept different types of marriages as easily as they accept later marriages now. Of course, I've never thought that my marriage was all that different. We love each other very much and we care deeply about each other's work. We share an awful lot. Maybe we don't eat breakfast together every morning, but at least we talk on the phone every day of our lives, no matter where we are, and we always know where we are, wherever we are, because where that place is is behind each other.

7 GROWING UP SUPPLEMENTAL

The trouble with being a prospect, female, growing up in Southern California, was that the Southern California Tennis Association was a regular male chauvinist den. That kind of thinking started with Perry Jones and with his right-hand man, Joe Bixler, the guy who succeeded him as head of the SCTA, and extended to Jack Kramer and his crowd, who played mostly at the Los Angeles Tennis Club, where the Association offices were located. There is a certain poetic justice that it was there, at the L.A. Tennis Club, where women's tennis was finally and absolutely forced to stand up for itself. When Kramer and his Pacific Southwest Tournament, which was played at the L.A. Tennis Club, offered the women such a piddling share of the purse in 1970, that was when we finally broke off on our own and attracted the support of Virginia Slims.

But in Southern California the boys invariably got all the

breaks. I can remember standing there on the sidelines at the L.A. Tennis Club, just drooling, watching Gonzales and Kramer and some of the other great players falling all over themselves to help Dennis Ralston improve his serve. I wanted to scream out, Just give me five minutes, five lousy minutes. . . . But of course, nobody bothered. If anybody had stopped to coolly, rationally examine little Billie Jean's chances and little Dennis's chances, they would have invested their time in me also, but girls were bush league, and so they kept working with Dennis, even though it was obvious that he was relatively limited on a world-class level.

Dennis wasn't dumb, either. He knew. He recognized his failings. Even then, when he was the number-one teenage prospect, when we would talk, he would tell me his dreams about becoming a fine coach someday. He knew he couldn't be a champion, and all the support given him simply served to put him under more pressure. "They're so high on me," he would say, "and I know I can't possibly live up to what they expect of me." After he and Rafe Osuna won the Wimbledon doubles in 1960, unseeded, all perspective on his future was lost. He would surely be the next Budge. The great irony was that it was Dennis, not all the Dennis-experts, who alone understood how good Dennis was.

In fact, Dennis did just about as well as should have been expected, given the fairly modest tools he had. He was just the best of a bad American lot at that time. The same thing with Arthur Ashe. You still hear so many people say that, with Arthur's big serve, if he had just had more killer instinct, why he would have won the Grand Slam year after year. Ridiculous. For a professional, Arthur was really a very average athlete. Ask him. He'll tell you that, even in his own family, his brother was a much better athlete.

But I would be unfair to all those dear folks in the Southern California Tennis Association if I left the impression that they were the only ones who discriminated against girl athletes.

Pretty much, in fact, the whole USLTA did. In those days, whatever your gender, the USLTA had to give you approval before you could play abroad. Then it would dish out some expense money. And one summer, when they doled out the grand sum of £100 to me, I knew they were giving Chuck McKinley £500. I knew. There aren't many secrets in tennis. They made the payoffs to us at Wimbledon in cash, in little white envelopes, right in the tea room. And I went to Bill Clothier, the big society honcho from Philadelphia, the *gentleman* who was in charge of that sort of thing, and I protested that it wasn't right that McKinley should get that much more—five times as much. It wouldn't have been so bad if Clothier could have at least stuck to his guns and said that he and the rest of the USLTA believed that women players were second-class citizens and we were lucky to get bus fare—at least I would have admired his honesty—but instead, he just lied outright and told me that I was mistaken and that McKinley certainly wasn't getting so much as a nickel more than I was.

The prejudice against female athletes was hardly confined to the old fuddy-duddies in tennis, either. It hurt me the most of all that my own school, Polytechnic, in Long Beach, never gave me any credit for what I accomplished. While I was still a student there, I was ranked as high as fourth in the country, but I was given little recognition there, in my own school. That was so painful for me. I think that the greatest time and place in all the world to be famous is when you're growing up, in your high school. And I never got any of that. And let me tell you this, too, that it doesn't matter how famous I became when I was a grown-up; that couldn't ever replace what I had missed when it mattered most. People always ask me if I'm not jealous of all the money that the kids make today, and sure, I'd like to get some of that, but I've learned to live with that fact. In fact, that's what I've fought for. But I'll tell you, what I'm really envious of is when I read that somebody like

Tracy or Andrea has gone back to their town or their school and they have been given a "day" or a parade in their honor.

I even remember one time when the junior high school principal—and she was a woman, too; I'll never forget her name: Jane Howard—wouldn't sign a lousy entry blank for me. It was permission to play in the Dudley Cup up in Santa Monica, which was a very crucial junior event in Southern California. The fee, all of three dollars, had been paid by the Long Beach Tennis Patrons, and the competition was scheduled so as not to conflict with school time. It was strictly a formality that the player's principal had to sign. But Jane Howard couldn't be bothered. It wasn't permitted by the school insurance contract, and it wasn't authorized for her in writing anywhere. She took no pride whatsoever that one of her students might bring the school some recognition and honor. I cried and cried, and finally, after days of browbeating her, she agreed to sign. Of course, afterward she never asked me how I had done.

Then in high school they would take the basketball team out and treat them all to steaks, but I wouldn't even be permitted time off from school. Finally, on one occasion, I took a half day off to play a match in the Pacific Southwest, and they gave me zeros for being absent. Then one day, when I was at Polytechnic, my brother came running home from Charles Evans Hughes Junior High (where I had gone to school before him), screaming, "Sis, Sis, they were showing your trophy today." They had finally put the trophy I had won at the Dudley Cup on display. Unfortunately, they never did anything like that when I was there. You see? Always the attention comes after you need it.

The funny thing was, of all the students at Polytechnic, the ones who best accepted me for my prowess in sports were the black guys, and, of course, they had no identification whatsoever with tennis. But even if they didn't know quite what it was I was doing, they understood the quality of my achievement and they always let me know that they were proud of me. One thing I've noticed, then and now: black men seem to be less prejudiced against female athletes than the whites. You were more likely to see a good black male athlete in school going out with a good black female athlete than to see that sort of romance between two whites. The white stars always wanted the cheerleaders instead. That may be changing at last, but maybe that's one reason why blacks produce such a disproportionate amount of top athletes: the best athletic genes are coming from both sides.

It wasn't just in high school where blacks were in my corner. All along, they seem to have identified with me more than most whites have. I think blacks see in me the same sort of qualities that they need to overcome the same sort of challenges. And boy, it was especially heartening right after the affair came out. Black people would call encouragement to me on the street, holler from cars, give me their salutes—everything.

In fact, a lot of blacks have told me that in many ways they can relate to me better than they can to Arthur. It isn't that they don't like him; on the contrary, they are extremely proud of what he has accomplished in a white man's sport. Instead, though, few of them on the street have any real sense of him. Arthur has become, in fact, something like Jackie Robinson—who is a man I have often been compared to, the analogy being that I accomplished for women in sports what Robinson did for blacks by breaking the racial barrier in the major leagues. But after Robinson left baseball he became an executive, living in the suburbs out of the black mainstream, so that the bulk of the black population simply lost touch with him.

Somebody even told me once, in fact, that in the numbers game in Harlem, zero had a code name of "Jackie Robinson." If, say, the winning number for the day was 407, a black man would say, "The number today was four–Jackie Robinson–

seven." It wasn't that they thought Robinson was a zero, a nothing; it was just that there was zero connection between them and him. And that is pretty much the way Arthur stands today for a lot of blacks.

As for me, what has bugged me about Arthur in the past is what a chauvinist pig he's been. He's always been capable of acknowledging some of us female athletes individually—I know he won some money betting on me against Bobby Riggs—but he has never really accepted women's tennis on equal footing with men's. Of course, Arthur's dearest friend is his lawyer, Donald Dell, who has been in league with Kramer for years and isn't much better on the subject of women and equal opportunity.

But I will give Arthur this: he seems to be coming around some since he got married. Jeanne, his wife, must be a very convincing person. He always told me that he would never marry a career woman—oh, he made a big point of that with me—but Jeanne is a very accomplished photographer, and perhaps she's making some impression on his old views.

Usually, too, I've noticed that it isn't wives who change men's opinions on the subject of women's rights. Men start to think more progressively only after they have a daughter and for the first time see how a girl—*their* little girl—can be denied. That's when a lot of men get some of that old-time feminist religion real fast.

But we surely could have used Jeanne Moutoussamy-Ashe working some magic on Arthur in 1973. That was the year that the men were threatening to boycott Wimbledon. The issue concerned the individual rights of players—their demand to act as private contractors and never mind what their national federations required. We might have become pros by this time, but in many respects we still had to go hat-in-hand to the Bill Clothiers of the tennis world and beg them for permission to play here or there. I've fought for this sort of thing all my life—and it had nothing to do with gender.

It did so happen, though, that at this time I was leading the movement to create the Women's Tennis Association—the last word being a polite euphemism for "union"—just as Ashe and several others of the men had spearheaded the formation of their Association of Tennis Professionals the September before. Never mind that the so-called Association of Tennis Professionals would not admit female tennis professionals; I went to Arthur and the other leaders of the ATP, and I told them, Look, we want to support you in this fight, so let's work together and if you do boycott Wimbledon, we're very likely to walk out with you. In fact, I personally promised that I would be in favor of such a move and would put both my name and energies behind it.

Now get the picture: the men have a dispute, and we are offering, free and clear, no strings attached, to stick our necks out and support them. Moreover, if we did, we would provide the men players with much more leverage. One of the reasons why Wimbledon eventually did endure the boycott so well was that the fans could at least be assured of seeing the regular women's field, even if the men's was cut down to a bunch of college kids and some Communists (Kodes of Czechoslovakia beat Metreveli of Russia in the final). So it was utterly in the men's self-interest to accept our assistance. And did they? They wouldn't even respond. I was never able so much as to get the ATP leaders to sit down and explore matters.

Because the ATP would not—if you will pardon the expression—get in bed with us, it made forming the Women's Tennis Association that much more difficult. The national federations were still very powerful, and several of the top players—Margaret Court, Virginia Wade, Evonne Goolagong—were, as always, afraid to take any risks. Also, there were a lot of fringe types who just couldn't understand why we should muddy the waters.

At the meetings at the Hotel Gloucester, no one was more of

a pain than Julie Anthony, who later became one of my very best friends. But at that time she was a no-risk college student taking summer vacation from Stanford, having a dandy time abroad, making a few bucks playing tennis. "But why should we have an Association?" she kept asking. "Why?"

Although it was a very sincere, good question, I still wanted to smash her and some of the others. In fact, Julie came up to me a few years later and said, "I must have been really difficult, wasn't I?"

And I said, "Yes."

But we got it through. The old National Tennis League alumnae—Rosie and Ann and Frankie and I—dredged up the votes. We were used to taking chances, we were the bravest, and we had the most street smarts. You know what the main problem was that we had to overcome? Women don't think conceptually very well. It was so hard for us to get the other players to visualize what an Association could mean. Now, please understand, I'm not suggesting that women are constitutionally weak in that manner of thinking. It is just the same old trap, that because we're not supposed to think that way, we're never trained to. But I fear it is so, nonetheless.

Luckily (thank you, Arthur), at Wimbledon in '73 we had the example of the ATP to show them—a clear reality, not a concept. And because of that, we prevailed and the WTA was founded. Also, we were very political. I hate anything to do with politics, but, you know, any port in a storm. For example, we made up a slate with Virginia as vice-president (and me as president), where she looked very prominent but didn't have anything to do. And eventually we got just about everybody who counted to go along, except for Evonne. To this day, I don't know why she didn't. To this day, I don't know why Evonne doesn't do a lot of things.

We came out of the meeting room at the Gloucester, and we were so excited. The press was all there, and I was shouting, "We did it! We did it! We have our Association!"

Wouldn't you know it? All anybody wanted to ask us was about how this related to the men's situation. "Are you going to boycott?" "Are you going along with the ATP?" Even when we formed a union, we had to be treated like the Ladies Auxiliary or the Junior League.

I was surprised one of the reporters didn't ask me about my hairdo or how I could expect to manage a marriage and a union at the same time.

On the other hand (deep sigh), when all is said and done, I would have to say that men have always understood me better than women. A simple example would be Ashe. Why did Arthur bet on me against Riggs? Because, he says, he was standing in the bar at (of all places) the Los Angeles Tennis Club, and he watched our first game on TV and he could see that, better than Bobby, I was moving well, I was hitting out with purpose, and Arthur understood what these characteristics meant, and he went with me. Men seem to be better able to see what constitutes me, and not just the end product.

All but one of the people who coached me was a man. And it is the men who most often seem able to relate me to their lives. Many women may think it's dandy what I stand for and how well I've done, but they can't translate that to their own experience.

My sister-in-law, Pam, Randy's wife, was explaining to me one day how her earnings as a flight attendant made for such a nice "supplementary income." Wait a minute! Red flag! I tried to explain to Pam that a dollar is a dollar is a dollar, whether Randy made it pitching or she did flying, and that, even beyond that, if she looked upon her dollars as supplementary, it was but a short step to thinking of herself as a supplementary person.

I can't tell you how many tennis cocktail parties I've had to attend over the years, when some cowering little thing approached me and told me how much she admired me and what an example I had served for her—and all the while identifying herself as "Joe Smith's wife."

"Yes, but who are you?" I would say.

And the answer would come back in more detail, but still in terms of her husband: "You know, Joe Smith, who you met—the assistant public-relations manager of Widget."

So, you see, I know in a lot of cases that I succeeded more in threatening weak men than in strengthening weak women.

Or take the case of someone smart and capable, like Edy McGoldrick, who worked for many years in positions of real authority for the United States Tennis Association—without pay. One day a few years ago, I asked Edy, "How many hours a week do you suppose you work?"

"Oh, at least forty," she said. "Maybe as much as sixty some weeks."

"Doesn't it ever bother you that you're not paid for all the work you do?"

"But we need volunteers, Billie Jean."

"Well, why should the volunteers always turn out to be women? Why should Mike Burns be paid?" (Mike is the executive secretary of the USTA.)

Edy was horrified. "But that's Mike's *job*!" she cried out.

"Well," I said, "what are your forty hours each week?"

"But I like what I'm doing."

"I'm sure Mike likes what he's doing, too. In fact, it's easier to like a job more when you're paid for it. Plus, you'll like yourself better." Edy still wasn't sure, so I went on. "Look at it this way, too. However you personally feel about working for free in this position, if you do, if you don't demand a fair salary, then you don't create anything for those who come after you."

And Edy went in the next day, asked for an appropriate figure, and walked right out with it. And subsequently she has gone on to positions of even greater authority as an independent promoter.

One of the main reasons why the old shamateurism game managed to survive despite all its deceits was that it was a system for introducing tennis-playing men into the business world. If you were polite and learned to dress right and had the correct manners, if you wrote prompt thank-you notes and made sure to talk to the ugly daughters of the right men at the club cocktail parties, then there might very well be a nice place in business for you. Overnight, you could go from tennis bum to weekend player.

But there was no Old Girl network to take care of the young women who came on the tour. Women can be so much better friends than can men, but women aren't conditioned to think in terms of helping each other along. That's why we're so vulnerable.

The spring of 1960, I was sixteen years old, ranked nineteenth in the country. My coach till then had been a wonderful old gentleman named Clyde Walker, and when I was suddenly given the opportunity to work every weekend with Alice Marble, I was scared that this move would offend Clyde. But on the contrary, when I went and told him, he was thrilled for me. All he could think was that Alice could help me in ways he couldn't. "That's the best possible thing for you at this time," he said. "Be around a real world champion. All I ever was was Texas State winner. There's aspects about playing at the top that I just can't even imagine."

And so, for really the only time in my life, I had a female mentor, the sort of rabbi that men pick up as a matter of course as they ascend any ladder. Alice lived alone in this nondescript little tract house up in Encino, an hour and a half away, and Mom would drive me up there every Saturday morning, then come back and pick me up Sunday night. That meant six hours for her on the road.

Alice was working in a doctor's office then. She had pleurisy, which had cost her one of her lungs, but she smoked all the time, coughing as she instructed me. What am I to say, because she's still alive twenty years later. The main thing Alice did was to help me to understand about how to win. And it was important to me that she wasn't just a champion talking to me—she was a *woman* who was a champion. For the first time in my life, I sensed some kind of legacy that I was part of. Now I really belonged to something. I went from number nineteen in the country up to number four that summer after Alice.

She was especially right for me, too, because she had played the same style as I did, serve-and-volley, which, of course, is fairly unusual among women. A few years before, someone had sent the young Maureen Connolly to Alice because Maureen was a backcourt player and Alice would be the perfect one to teach her to serve. But it didn't work that way. They didn't understand one another. But Alice and I thought alike. In fact, the funny thing was that what Alice helped me the most with was groundstrokes. We could relate to each other in our whole style, so that we could understand each other well in any detail in the mosaic. She kept rasping at me that I was too close to the ball when I hit a groundstroke, that almost all players stood too close because they were insecure and afraid to move away. I was lucky. I knew baseball well, and so I could envision hitting a ball out over the far corner of the plate. She knew baseball, too. As a little girl she had been the mascot for the San Francisco Seals.

Then nights we would just sit around talking. Alice had a great sense of humor; she was really alive. She had been kind of a Hollywood tennis darling for a while, and she would tell me stories about Gable and Lombard and all those stars, and then she would take out the guitar and sing for me. She could really sing. She sang some songs in Spanish, and there were pictures of her around of her singing professionally. I remember one from a New York hotel. So Alice would sing and smoke, and I would read through all her scrapbooks. Boy, did I eat it up. I was in seventh heaven.

And then one night she asked me what my goal in tennis was, and I said it was to be the best in the world. I meant it just for myself. I mean, I was still just a high-school kid and I didn't even think of myself in her terms. But she took it, somehow, as me wanting to surpass her, and she got furious. She screamed at me. She called me "you ungrateful brat," and the next night, when my mother came up to Encino, I said good-bye to Alice. I couldn't understand why she was so cruel to me, and years later, after I won Wimbledon, she wrote me a lovely letter. Maybe it was just that she couldn't do any more for me, but she didn't know how to round things off. It doesn't matter, anyway, because even if Alice hurt me for the moment, she had been so important to me. I had needed to meet a woman who was a champion, who was a living and breathing vision of what I wanted to be.

A few months ago, Helen Reddy, the singer, invited me to a luncheon one afternoon at her house. There were show-biz women, executives, judges, politicians. I knew I was probably an afterthought, but okay, you have to start somewhere. And everybody was delighted to meet me, and the conversation was fascinating, although at some point somebody had to bring up the Riggs match and everybody had to tell me where they had been that night. But this happens all the time. Everybody I meet has a compulsion to tell me where exactly they were when I beat Bobby, even though 99 percent of the time it is just that they were in front of this television set or that one. When I die, at my funeral, nobody's going to talk about me. They're all just going to stand up and tell each other where they were the night I beat Bobby Riggs.

But anyway, at the meeting, after a while we began to talk more seriously about sports, and I turned to former Congresswoman Bella Abzug, and I said, "You know, the real shame is that women's sports could be so visible. It is such an obvious tool. But you've never used it. No one has."

And she agreed. Women executives have never supported women's sports, while their male counterparts are always helping men's sports. I believe, though, that the new generation of female leaders will understand about women's sports and use them. I do think things are changing. The hardest thing about being a woman in a man's world was not just that it was lonely, that you felt so out of place. What was really depressing was that you knew you could never look back for help, because none was coming. Now, at last, it is.

8 STARTING WITH CHRIS AND JIMMY

I was ranked nationally in 1959 by the USLTA, and as late as 1981 I was ranked by the WTA computer, so I can claim that I played world class in four different decades. As long as that sounds, though, it seems even longer because I bridged whole eras. Playing back in the fifties and early sixties had much more in common with the twenties and thirties than it did with the years immediately following.

So many of the girls playing today are like aliens to me, and I'm sure I'm even more foreign to them, because in all the ways that we differ, where we are most apart is with tradition. The players today have almost no sense of history. They don't feel part of anything grand or dear or lasting. As a matter of fact, most of them pretty much accept it that tennis began with Chris Evert on the women's side and Jimmy Connors on the men's. Our Adam and Eve. Oh sure, literally the players recognize that something came back there before

Chris and Jimmy, but whatever it was, it doesn't really matter.

I was talking one day with Ann Kiyomura, who is a bright young person I like, and I said, "Ever read any books about tennis?"

She looked at me like I was crazy. "Why would I do that?" she said. "I play tennis."

By the time I was Ann's age, I had read everything about tennis that I could get my hands on, and since the only books I could find about women's tennis were Alice Marble's *The Road to Wimbledon* and *Tennis with Hart*, by Doris Hart, I had just about committed them to memory.

Alice Marble? Doris Hart? Louise Brough? Pauline Betz? Who in the world are they? When Chris walked into the little ready room they have at Wimbledon just before her 1981 final with Hana Mandlikova, Hana spotted a picture on the wall and asked who it might be. Chris was flabbergasted. "That's Maureen Connolly," she said. And then she realized that she might as well have said "Marie Antoinette" for all that meant to Hana.

I know I'm the next one on the way out, too. A friend told me that my name came up in the locker room at Wimbledon last year, and one of the younger players, Ros Fairbank, said, "Didn't she win here a couple of times?"

At one WTA meeting we gave a seminar on handling finances. Next time, I think we should require attendance at a lecture on the history of women's tennis. All of this lack of interest in the game's past especially upsets me because, notwithstanding all the misconceptions about my being a wild-eyed revolutionary, anxious to lay waste to all treasured institutions, I actually see myself as very much a traditionalist. I think when you come from a strong and secure family background, you develop a confidence within yourself about what is best to be kept, but also what can be changed. Here is a favorite quotation of mine, from e. e. cummings, that applies so well to me: "As it was my miraculous good fortune to have a true father and a true mother, and a home which the truth of their love made joyous, so—in reaching outward from this love and this joy—I was marvellously lucky to touch and seize a rising and striving world; a reckless world, filled with the curiosity of life herself; a vivid and violent world welcoming every challenge; a world worth hating and adoring and fighting and forgiving; in brief, a world which was a world."

Ultimately, I wanted tennis changed because I loved tennis so much and wanted all of it as good for everyone as the parts that were already so good for me.

The horrible thing I feel about some of the younger players today is not merely that they lack a devotion to the history of the game, but that they have so little curiosity about anything around them. So much has been given them that they tend to accept everything at face value. And for all their money—boy, are most of them cheap. The Aussies had an expression for it: "short arms, long pockets." Ken Rosewall—"Muscles"—was Exhibit A. It was supposed to be the crowning accomplishment of my career with the National Tennis League that he volunteered to take me out to dinner after practice one night—and not only sprung for the best of the menu, but also for a good bottle of wine. But to give Muscles his due, he was simply very frugal. A lot of the young players today are uncaring, generally inconsiderate.

When Larry promotes a tournament now, he writes into the budget $250 for towels that some of the kids will just take with them and then leave in cabs or hotel rooms. Worse, he also budgets about $300 for tips that he leaves at the tournament hotel for the bellhops and maids. With the hundreds of thousands of dollars that the players make now, they stiff the help.

It is also increasingly difficult to count on the young players for the tedious obligations that go with the game: posing

for publicity photos, attending sponsor parties, making appearances to hype a tournament—all that sort of thing that
no pro has ever enjoyed doing. The only difference is, we put
on our makeup and gritted our teeth and did it. The kids
today forget or oversleep or just plain tell you to stick it. What
do they care? Tennis has forever been a golden goose—
right?—and it will go on this way forever.

Through my generation, players were intimately involved
in the business end of the game. Many of the best players—
like my pals Riggs and Kramer—ran their own tours. And the
rest of us, like Ann and Rosie and Frankie and me, at least
knew the business end. The players today have no real interest in where their prize money is coming from and, in fact,
often tend to look upon the promoters as suckers and adver-
saries, rather than as our partners.

I remember a year or so ago, at a board meeting of the
WTA, when we were discussing the very sensitive issue of
whether or not we should raise the fees that we charge
tournament promoters by 5 percent. As I pointed out, the
WTA needed the extra income, yet we had to be careful
because even the 5 percent might be a large additional expense for a lot of loyal tournament promoters. I was stunned
at the antagonistic response, and one of the players actually
piped up and said, "So who cares if the promoters lose
money?"

I will say this for the present crop, that they are deprived in
one way: they don't have the camaraderie that we enjoyed.
We were bound together in so many ways. First of all, we
always felt like underdogs—as tennis players and as women
athletes. So we tended to be defensive and stuck together for
mutual support. Secondly, our world was structured more
simply. There was one main tour, and it played country clubs
during the days. Our nights were free, so we had a much more
agreeable social life. But particularly as the open era struggled to find itself, we caucused all the time for serious pur-

poses. It was like that old joke: "What's the difference between drunks and alcoholics? Drunks don't have to go to meetings." We were always meeting. We were competitors on the court, friends off, and business partners always. Women's tennis is so fragmented today, and with all the parents and coaches traveling now, the sense of belonging that we had is fading all the more.

The terrible thing is, too, that the men players have an even worse reputation for being cavalier and uncaring. I mean, they really take the money and run. The few men who show any responsibility tend to be the old-timers, of my generation, who came up through the shamateurism game, who've seen the bad and the good and appreciate how lucky we are now. But there's not many of us left, male or female, with that perspective. Besides, as the players on tour grow younger, there is a general diminution in maturity. When the WTA was founded in 1973, our median age was twenty-six. In less than a decade it has dropped down to twenty-two, and our members are as young as fourteen. No matter how advanced those kids are as athletes, how can they be expected to understand issues and to make responsible decisions?

Another thing: the women are becoming more and more like the men. Now I know this is going to break a few hearts, because it is an article of faith that if we can just get more women out there—with our warm maternal instincts—running the world, then it will quickly all be hearts and flowers, peace and justice throughout the world, starting promptly the day after tomorrow. But everything that I see in tennis suggests the contrary: that if you place women in the positions of prominence and power traditionally held by men, it is not the position that changes, it is the woman. Remember that old husbands' tale: the office makes the woman.

As a promoter, Larry can see clearly how the ladies are beginning to resemble the gentlemen. For example, right up until 1980, we could always deliver a guaranteed number of our drawing cards and stars to our women's tournaments, but recently, for the first time, some of the big names have refused to play in their quota of tournaments. In some cases this has meant a reduction in overall prize money. But the stars can still make theirs on the side, from endorsements and exhibitions. And this, of course, is precisely the attitude that most of the male stars have exhibited for years now, to the detriment of the whole game.

To me, what this proves, above all, is what I've always said: that women aren't any better than men, but that we're all siblings under the skin. I only maintained that we should have the opportunity to be as rotten and venal as men. And now that we've been given the chance, we're coming through with flying colors. In fact, I would suggest that in tennis (and possibly in other sports as well) women are every bit as tough as competitors as the men. If not more so.

I really had to laugh when I played in a special team competition in Turin a while ago, and the little Italian promoter, who had run men's tournaments before, was incredulous when we kept playing well past the dinner hour. "I can't believe you girls!" he screamed. "You don't tank. And all the men tank. I can't believe you!"

And after all, female athletes are more likely to grow up trying to prove something. In this sense, we are more like a minority male athlete, a black or Hispanic. In addition, we have the added burden of lacking approval from much of society. At least a black male athlete gets plenty of cultural reinforcement, whereas female athletes are still too often viewed as mannish freaks. So, yes, we are out to prove something, and it is starting to show.

Most people—men, especially—missed the point when Pam Shriver lost her temper after Tracy Austin beat her in the summer of 1981 in Toronto. Pam came to the net and screamed at Tracy, and of course this titillated everybody when they discovered the four-letter words that Pam had chosen. Everybody kept saying that it showed that the women players were just like the men. But that misses the point. It wasn't just that Pam said some dirty words—big deal. No, it was that she directed them at an opponent.

I certainly don't condone what Pam did. In fact, I feel very sorry for her because from my own past experience I know how hard it is to live down an incident like this. She is going to pay for it. She'll be asked about it for as long as she plays. But what I am trying to point out is how intense and competitive we weaker sex have become out there.

A happier illustration of the same point occurred one night in the summer of 1981 when Barbara Potter was playing singles in Team Tennis against my club, Oakland. I was supposed to meet her in singles that night, but I was injured and Ann Kiyomura substituted. Pottsy beat Ann, and right after she won the match she came storming over to our bench, stood right in front of me, pointed a finger in my face, and screamed, "I want *you* now!"

I mean, this was vintage Muhammad Ali. Phil Dent was sitting next to me, and he was horrified. He'd never seen anything like this in men's. I had to put a hand on his shoulder to reassure him. He was ready to jump up and grab Pottsy.

Keep in mind, too, that we are not talking about some crazy last-chance ghetto kid. Pottsy's father is an artist, and she attended prep school at Taft, where she graduated near the top of her class, and was accepted by Princeton. She is so bright and mature, a voracious reader—I always tell her that she's nineteen going on forty-five—and here she is so keyed up that she's yelling at me, threatening me. Terrific! I love it!

So many of the kids are like that. You go to press conferences today and you won't hear any of that foolishness that you used to, about how I was fortunate to win, the other player just had some bad luck—all that garbage. Now the girls speak right up and admit that they want to win, tell how much winning means to them, and how they hate to lose. As a matter of fact, I find that often they are too insensitive with victory. If they beat a player who is out there with a hundred and one temperature or a bad leg or jet lag, there is never any sympathy or accommodation. A win is just a big W, and no questions asked.

Pottsy is not all that unusual in her background, either. It is still difficult for the players—of either sex—who do not come from wealthy backgrounds to make it in tennis, and an inordinate number of pros came up through country clubs and prep schools. But don't stereotype them; they're a different breed of cat.

For example, as I mentioned, the man who really taught me the game was a great old gentleman named Clyde Walker. He had spent almost all of his career working at country clubs, but shortly before I dropped into his life he had quit club coaching to take a job in the Long Beach Recreation Department because he felt that he would never find anyone at a club with the grit to become a champion. He thought he would have a better chance in the public parks, and of course he was proved right because not only did I come along but so did a fine boy player, Jerry Cromwell.

But I was a real fluke. Clyde had to coach at all the various parks in Long Beach, giving his clinics each day at a different court, like some kind of old circuit-riding judge. The park where he met me was Houghton, where he taught Tuesdays. But he was amazed to find me at another park, miles away, the next day, and a third park the day after that, and so on. "What *are* you doing here?" he asked me.

"Mr. Walker, I can't get any good at this game if I only get lessons once a week," I said. But how many kids would understand that?

The rich kids in the game today had it a lot more convenient than I did, that's for sure, but I see in them the same kind of determination. They're sort of hybrids. On the one hand, they're very modern, very spoiled, but on the other hand, they all seem to be imbued with the good old-fashioned Protestant work ethic. And they're specialists—very single-minded, as you must be. It sounds contradictory, but their parents have spoiled them and disciplined them, alike.

Everybody makes a big fuss about how little Czechoslovakia has produced so many champions recently, of both sexes, and all the articles on the subject have pointed out how the Czechs run such an organized state system, wherein the best prospects are identified at the earliest age and then given the best coaching. That's all true enough, too, but what everyone has failed to see is that if you look closely you will see that all these good Czech players—Navratilova and Mandlikova and Ivan Lendl at the top, down to Renata Tomanova and Helena Sukova and Tomas Smid and some others in the second rank—all of them had enthusiastic, athletic parents who supported them. Just like the Americans.

The British are always complaining that they don't have the proper facilities to produce champions, but Larry was the first one to convince me that that excuse is a cop-out. Champions are not produced by good facilities. It's more the other way around. If your country or your area produces a champion, then that might result in better facilities being built, and a greater chance for a second generation of top players to be developed.

The British aren't failing to produce top tennis talent because they lack good facilities. The British lack the right attitudes and role models. They are failing because they still think like r/u's and they celebrate r/u's. But I think change is coming there, and to a lot of other countries, because I think these nationalities have seen how tough our young American players are and how much we care about winning, and so they're starting to emulate us. Anne Hobbs and Sue Barker are perfect examples of how foreign players will change outlook after they have been around American players for a while. They no longer have that typical British r/u mentality. And certainly the track stars Sebastian Coe and Steve Ovett have had a positive influence.

Recently a lot of experts have expressed concern that Americans were beginning to dominate what has always been such a wonderful international sport, and possibly for the immediate future, the next couple years, Americans will win even more in tennis. But then I think the pendulum will begin to swing back because as the other players start to copy our competitiveness they will begin to beat us at our own game.

On the women's side I think we have more of an edge, though, because however much there may be sexual inequality in America, we are certainly more enlightened than the rest of the world. Nowadays, some of the young American girls I meet tell me they were introduced to tennis by their mothers—in the same way that so many fathers and sons have shared sports. It used to be, too, that it was more often the father who introduced his daughter to the sport—Chris, of course, being the classic example.

Or even me. When I was four, I begged my father to play some ball with me, and then after a while I begged him to buy me a baseball bat, and while he said he couldn't afford to buy me a bat, he carved one for me. I was so excited hitting the ball for the first time that I threw the bat down and ran inside to get my mother. If this was so much fun, then I wanted her to come out and join in. But she turned me down. "No, thank you, dear, my fingernails might break," she said.

My mother was no wimp. She was a good athlete, a fine swimmer and dancer. But her response on that occasion was probably predictable for that time and place. Dad is the one who was supposed to play ball. But now, as more and more mothers play sports and encourage their daughters to play them, then that is bound to weave female athletics into our broad cultural fabric and produce more quality players.

And I'll say this for today's younger players: they work.

They will stand out there on the practice courts and hit ball after ball, grooving in, for hours. In 1978, when we were playing the Federation Cup in Madrid, Tracy Austin came to me and said she *had* to work out at eight the next morning. Eight o'clock—that was her routine. I was sick as a dog with my usual bronchitis or whatever, coughing up all kind of junk, and Connie Spooner, our trainer, was sick with the same sort of thing, but we struggled out of bed so that Tracy could have her workout. Now, I will say this for Tracy: that later on she figured out how demanding she had been, that life on a team is not quite the same as when you have your mother and coach at your beck and call, and she did apologize. But the point is that the way these kids are brought up, they practice all the time and they expect to have someone to hit with them.

You know where I see something very similar to tennis practice? Those electronic pinball games. The players—girls and boys alike—all stand there, throwing quarters in and playing Space Invaders or whatever, hour after hour. I really believe these games make it easier for kids to be more competitive and concentrated out on the court. I'm serious. If you could just see Tracy or Andrea Jaeger or some of these others shooting down spaceships, you would understand completely when you saw them standing behind the baseline and crunching the balls deep into the corners.

But the trouble with the way these younger players practice is that it is too mechanical, that there is no real thoughtful design to it. I mean, Tracy would ask me to get up and hit with her at eight, but she had no idea what to ask me to hit her. Of course, you can say, Well, she won the U.S. Open twice and she's just nineteen, so how can you quibble? And if you would say that, it would be hard for me to argue with you. Still, as well as Tracy strokes, she does not yet play the game anywhere near as well as she can. And Andrea is simply never going to become a champion unless she learns to emphasize

some part of her game. No player, male or female, has ever
become truly great without having one stroke to depend on.
Andrea must learn to make the big, killing shot, but instead,
every time she has the chance to penetrate naturally, she
draws back, retreating to the baseline and sameness. It
sounds so foolish to say when she is still barely seventeen, but
the next year or two are going to be crucial to her development. If she doesn't show something new, the other players
will be after her like sharks.

The two players from my general era who are the most
bitter about the game today—about the way the players are,
their attitude, their money, all that—are Rosie Casals and
Roy Emerson. It may mean something, too, that they were
both such popular players—everybody loved Emmo, the life
of every party, and everybody loved little Rosie and wanted
to take care of her.

It especially bugs Emmo that Bjorn Borg can win so regularly on grass and other fast surfaces. "Nobody can hit a
bloody first volley at all," Emmo cries out. "So they let Borg
stand back there and hit groundstrokes on grass."

And, of course, he's right. Borg can't hit an effective first
volley, either, and neither does any other man around today,
except perhaps McEnroe; now, I think, his volley even stacks
up against people like Laver and Roche. But it is also true
that the players today are so much faster, and they come over
the ball so well and give it so much more spin, that

1. it's a whole lot harder now to knock off that first volley
just like you want to; and

2. even if you hit an excellent one, a deep shot that would
have been a sure winner once upon a time, your opponent
might run it down.

So maybe the reason nobody hits good first volleys anymore is not that they're dumb and uninvolved, but that, like
the natural selection of the species, it has just come to be
instinctively understood that first volleys don't count all that

much anymore and therefore they have sort of died a natural death of attrition.

The trouble is, human nature being what it is, our memories distort and we all want to think that our prime was the best old time of all. I'm hardly out of the game, and already I find myself celebrating the good old days, when players were players and first volleys were first volleys. I told Larry once, I made him promise, that if whenever I got old and he heard me babbling on about me and my time being the golden age, he was to do one thing: wherever we were, whatever the circumstance, no matter who we were with, he was to stand back and kick me right square in the rear end.

9 FLAT EYES AND BAHOOLAS

It's really impossible for athletes to grow up. As long as you're playing, no one will let you. On the one hand, you're a child, still playing a game. And everybody around you acts like a kid, too. But on the other hand, you're a superhuman hero that everyone dreams of being. No wonder we have such a hard time understanding who we are. But either way, you see, the usual response is to spoil the athlete—child or god.

And you learn very quickly that everything has a trade-off. "Let me get you a towel. . . ." "Can I give you a ride over? It's not *that* far out of the way. . . ." "Look, I'd love to get you in on this deal. . . ." Everything is Brownie points, for autographs or time or access or some other favor. You're always special, always the center of attention, always the topic of discussion. No wonder it's so hard for most athletes to cut and run, to enter the real world.

Actually, too, I surely had a more independent athletic

upbringing than most all other pros. The younger players on the tour today have coaches or parents traveling with them all the time, and so they're completely insulated from the inconveniences of the real everyday existence that the rest of us must deal with. In team sports, players have everything taken care of by trainers and team secretaries. Sports is full of stories of grown men who had been in the major leagues for years but didn't know how to claim their luggage or check into a hotel room when suddenly they had to take a trip on their own. I can believe it. When I first started traveling with World Team Tennis, I couldn't believe how much was done for you. Our trainer, Lou del Collo, took care of everything. It was great!

So, as Larry will tell you, for all my maturity and focus, I was a baby to start with and tennis has helped keep me one. I really never changed that much in what I did, how I acted. The most apparent change I ever made was to stop chattering to myself on the court. Oh, I might still call myself names and scream out in frustration, but after I lost that Forest Hills final to Margaret Smith in 1965, I figured it was time to stop having running conversations with myself. It was natural for me to chatter out there, and everybody thought it was so cute and loved it, but it was obviously distracting me. So, I became more boring, but more of a winner. Unfortunately, I'm afraid that's the way it must be in any technique sport.

The other thing I noticed was that my temper got worse over the years. That's a sure sign to get out. Mostly what sets you off is the frustration. All of a sudden, you can't quite do what you could just manage to do this time last year, and it's very confusing to you, and it doesn't seem fair, after all the work you've put into something, that all of a sudden your body won't allow you to do something, even as you've gotten smarter and know what to do. So, you throw a fit. What else? In that sense, it is the rare athlete who doesn't become more of a child, the older he or she gets.

They always say the legs go first. And the eyes, too. And then all the other players notice, and they pick on your weakness all the more, and you spiral down even faster and get angrier and act even more childish.

In many ways, for all my athletic instincts and God-given abilities, I shouldn't have been an athlete. I'm really too mercurial to be one; I'm too up and down. I can go, for easiest example, twenty pounds one way or the other in the space of a year. That's ridiculous. I decided once that my best playing weight was one hundred and thirty-three, but that was like Shangri-la. In any case, I was never there. I eat all the wrong things. I like every kind of junk food, Mexican food—tacos! talk to me!—Italian food. I adore sugar. Fritz Buehning says I need "a sugar buzz." I adore bagels. For some reason, I took up drinking coffee at the age of twenty-eight and now I'm a caffeine-aholic. Well, one thing: I hardly ever touch any liquor at all, and I've never missed that.

As a matter of fact, I'm pretty Calvinistic when it comes to pleasures. I think you must earn your highs, whether that means hitting some fantastic backhand down the line on break point, or making love with the man you love on a soft night under a full moon in Kauai. To go out and buy some stuff and sniff it up your nose and feel artificially good that way—that just isn't *right* to me. That's really being spoiled. How can anything mean anything to you if you don't at least have to help create the experience yourself?

The most obvious reason why I shouldn't have been an athlete is my eyes: 20/400. I started wearing glasses at the age of thirteen, after I'd been playing tennis for a couple of years. It was incredible. I could see the ball—imagine! Everybody else in my family has good eyes, too; Randy has absolutely outstanding vision. But here's the anomaly: even if I have bad eyes, I have a very good eye—you know, hand/eye coordination. Vic Braden has all these tests that prove, he says, that no one can possibly follow the ball all the way to where it actually touches the racket face, and I swear by almost everything Vic says about tennis, but I'm still not absolutely convinced that I haven't been able to see the ball hit the racket.

The main difficulty with having to wear glasses is that my perspiration from my forehead and hair gets on them, especially when I have to turn my head quickly. And when you wear glasses, you must turn your whole head more in order to see the ball. You can't just dart over with your eyes or your eyes will dart out the side of the glasses and you won't see anything. I tried wearing contacts, but it turns out that I am twice cursed with flatness—also in my eyes. Probably unless you have them yourself you never knew there was a thing such as flat eyes, but that is the case with certain people, and for whatever the technical reasons, it makes it difficult to keep contacts in place. I will say this, too: that one brief period when I wore contacts was enough to show me how much better you can see the ball with them.

Ironically, though, for as long as I played, I never really felt that my vision seriously affected the outcome of any match I was in until virtually the last important one I played. That was my last singles match at Wimbledon, the quarterfinals against Martina in 1980. We started late in the afternoon on a cold, drizzly day. The weather had been terrible all along, and the tournament was behind in its schedule, so they begged us to go on. I agreed, but I made them promise that if it started to drizzle again, the match would be stopped. Of course, Mrs. King, they said; thank you for your cooperation. And it started near the end of the first set. I reminded the chair umpire that they had promised not to make me play in any rain, but all the high officials had gone somewhere where it was nice and dry and warm and couldn't be found. I was up 5–1 in the tiebreaker, but my glasses were all wet, and Martina came back and won the set. Then they called the match for the night.

The next morning, before we resumed play, I noticed in the locker room that Rosie was just about to sit down in the chair where I had laid my glasses. I stopped her, and then I said, "Don't worry, it wouldn't have mattered, because I always have a spare." And then I stopped and said, "And you know, it's funny, all these years I've never needed that spare."

Well, wouldn't you know. When we started, I just ran through Martina 6–1 to tie the match, but at 9–8 in the final set, during a crossover, I took my glasses off to wipe my face, and when I put them back on, the sidepiece just came off in my hands. And so I had to turn to the spare, and even though it was a duplicate, no two pair of glasses ever feel the same, and Martina finally beat me 10–8. I think that may be the single match in my career that I could have won if I hadn't had bad eyes.

That was a very unpredictable Wimbledon, too. Martina then lost to Chris in three sets in the semis—neither one of them playing especially well—and after that, Evonne upset Chris in the final. I always wanted that one last Wimbledon after I un-retired, and that one was obviously my best chance.

If there was one advantage to wearing glasses, it was that everybody always told me how I couldn't possibly become a champion wearing them, and that only got my back up and made me all the more determined. At that time, when I first appeared on the scene, I think that the only player of any consequence ever to have worn glasses was Jaroslav Drobny. Ashe did later, and so did an old gentleman named Riggs. One thing that is nice, too: I regularly get letters from parents telling me how their son or daughter who wears glasses doesn't feel quite so much like old four-eyes because of what I have accomplished.

Through the years, a much greater drawback than my eyes was the general state of my health, especially my respiratory system. I'm just a wreck. I have some form of bronchitis or asthma, and I often experience difficulty in breathing. In fact, the way it occasionally worked out was that it would take a while for my lung passages to clear out and I would literally get a second breath well into a match. England was always the worst place on earth for me, except possibly airplanes (if they count as on earth). I always have to wear long-sleeved blouses and sweaters on planes because they're so cold, and the air is so dry that even a short flight has been enough to really wipe me out.

I don't think that I was ever truly healthy for a Wimbledon. The last time I won, in 1975, I had a temperature that stayed around a hundred and two and a low-grade infection that hung on throughout the fortnight. But then, whenever I get a cold it takes forever for me to shake it off. Sometimes, in fact, I don't think I've ever had a completely healthy day since I had all those problems in '75. But before now, I've never talked about all my pulmonary problems, because I believe in the old Aussie spirit: that if you go out on that court to play, then you're well. No excuses, mate.

I'm a trouper. I'm a pro. I take great pride in being a professional, and I hate the word "amateur." Professional to me means, above all, being highly skilled at something; only secondarily does it mean getting paid. The point was so effectively made in *Chariots of Fire*, perhaps my all-time favorite movie, which was ostensibly about amateur athletics.

So, you pay the price. Everything is a give-and-take. As much as I hate having to get in a plane and go places, I do love it when I get there. So many American players are so parochial. I think the British took to me so quickly because they recognized right away that I liked being there. I enjoyed being someplace different from Long Beach, California, U.S.A. You know, when I was a little girl and we had a twenty-minute recess each morning, your own time, I would often just go up to the world map by myself and stare at all the places that I wanted to visit.

My first airplane trip was in 1959, eleven hours in a Constellation, across the country to Philadelphia. I loved it! I had to sit next to Carole Caldwell, and when the trip started, I really didn't like her, but by the time we landed we were the best of friends. And Philadelphia, the East Coast—back East!—it just blew my mind. I couldn't believe that anything could be so green. I had never seen anything like those magnificent trees in Chestnut Hill, where we stayed with a family named the Freunds. I know that Californians can be the pickiest people of all, especially when it comes to the weather, but not me, not ever. I'm so very American in most ways, but like all the foreign kids who learn to adapt to different cultures, I was always able to adjust—and don't think that isn't important if you want to succeed in an international sport.

The funniest part about my first trip East was after we left Philadelphia and went to stay at Margaret Osborne duPont's mansion in Wilmington, Delaware. She had been champion at both Wimbledon and Forest Hills and was my favorite Wightman Cup captain. We'd been living in some pretty fancy houses in Philly, but for a little fireman's daughter, the duPonts' was something out of a fairy tale. "Karen, look!" I cried. "This bathroom is larger than our whole house." And then we both broke up altogether when Mr. duPont asked if we'd like to see the rest of the place, and we said sure, and he said, "Well, let's get in the car." Imagine having to drive to the rest of the house! And it was this cheap little six-cylinder standard-shift Chevy. When we had dinner, there were maids and butlers who passed trays for us to serve ourselves off of. I'd never done that in my life. Either Mom put the plate on the table or we helped ourselves. To this day, wherever I am, if I have to serve myself at my place, I flash back to "duPont" in my mind and get scared all over again that I'm going to spill everything in my lap. You can take the girl out of Long Beach, but . . .

In those days of the amateurs, of course, it was the normal routine to be put up with families at a tournament. It was known simply as "housing" or staying "with people." (Some players still prefer that, too. Betty Stove, for example, will always stay *with people* instead of at a hotel if she possibly can.) At first I just accepted this arrangement, and I even enjoyed meeting all kinds of people, but later I came to question it because I realized it was just additional evidence of how bush tennis was. I could imagine the Chicago White Sox landing in Boston and the players fanning out all over the city, staying with people. I remember that when the Virginia Slims circuit got off the ground what made me happiest, what really told me that we were for real, that we were pros, that we were big league, was that we stayed in Holiday Inns.

But then, maybe it was best for me at first to be thrown in with strangers. I grew up in a very sheltered way (as most of us do), and being exposed to different people with different attitudes at an early age was crucial to my broadening development. I can freeze up when I'm forced to be on display, and in company I don't like I can even get claustrophobic, but in a small circle, in a house, then I'm able to feel at home. Larry even says he can tell what sort of people I've been with from the expressions I use. I like colorful words that really connect people. I pick up expressions like a furry dog going through a burr patch. But I'm always loyal to my all-time, old-time favorites, too: waffles, blebs, blubbergut, from Shinola, mombotious, talk to me, turkey, you got to love it, wazoo, and bahoola. I guess that's number one on the hit parade: bahoola. My father used to always say it. It means your rear end. Bust your bahoola. Every now and then I heard that the writers would get up a pool on how many times I would say "bahoola" in a press conference. Those turkeys!

One of my favorite housings I ever had was with the Brennans, in New Jersey. Frank and Lillian had ten kids— ten, count 'em, ten—and he somehow managed as a tennis coach back before the tennis boom. The first time I ever met

him was that first summer in the East, when I was fifteen and
fat and wearing rhinestone glasses that were broken and held
together by a safety pin. But I took Maria Bueno to three sets,
and Mr. Brennan was able to look past my appearance, and
he came right up to me afterward and introduced himself
and, flat-out, he told me, "Don't worry, you're gonna be
number one someday." I was stunned. That was the first time
anybody had ever said anything like that to me.

And then Mr. Brennan checked out my rackets. I only had a
couple free Wilsons, strung with nylon, which is about half as
cheap as real gut, which any real player would use. I told him
that was all I could afford, and he told me not to worry, he
could get me some cut-rate gut from Pakistan. From Pakistan—it sounded like some spy movie to me.

But thereafter I always stayed with the Brennans when I
was playing in the area. You had to fight tooth and nail with
their brood for your dinner, but it was worth it. Where Mr.
Brennan was so helpful to me was in terms of strategy, and
believe me, that is a real bonus ever to have anyone like that.
The longer I stayed in tennis, the more amazed I was at how
very few people really understood how the game works.

Mr. and Mrs. Brennan came over with Larry and me to
Wimbledon in 1967, and we all stayed in the Hotel Lexham,
off Cromwell Road. Then, the day before I was to play in all
three finals—singles, doubles, and mixed—Mr. Brennan suddenly had a massive coronary and had to be rushed to the
hospital. Larry kept the news from me until I came off the
court, and then I went directly to the hospital.

While worrying about Mr. Brennan, I couldn't help but
hearking back six years before that, to another Wimbledon
and another coach, Clyde Walker. He had developed cancer,
and even before I left for England he was in the hospital, on
the verge of death. But Clyde hung on, and although I was
beaten in the singles, Karen Hantze and I started to move
through the draw in the doubles, and every day it would
make his day to read that we had won again.

It was crazy. Karen and I were teenagers, completely unseeded, and we had only played a couple of warm-up tournaments together. The way we decided that she would take the
backhand court was to flip a coin—a real sophisticated team.
But we were so completely loose, Karen told me all along
we'd win, and we did keep on winning and got to the finals.
And Clyde Walker wouldn't die, even though none of the
doctors understood how he stayed alive. And for the finals, we
played the Aussies, Margaret Smith and Jan Lehane, who
made up one of the best teams in the world, but we beat them,
too, and Karen and I were world champions.

That night, they came into his room at the hospital and
said, "Clyde, Billie Jean won," and he smiled. He died the
next day. All he ever wanted was to coach a world champion.

So, naturally, I thought all about this when Frank Brennan
went into the hospital, but I went out the next day and played
all three finals, and won all three. And in Mr. Brennan's case
there was a happy ending, too, because he recovered—and,
for that matter, he's still alive and kicking today.

The year before, 1966, when I won my first singles at
Wimbledon, Larry and I also stayed at the Lexham. I'll bet
my digs that year were as primitive as they come. We stayed
in Room 33, without a bathroom. We had to go down the hall
to use a community toilet.

I played Bueno in the final. Everybody loved to watch
Maria because she was so graceful, even more balletic than
Goolagong, I would say, because Maria had much longer, real
showgirl legs. And she had magnificent court presence. She
would thrive even more today, with all the greater publicity
and attention. I mean, Maria was a real star turn. She even
kept herself aloof from the rest of the players, which added to
her aura, and along with her height and her big serve, it
helped her to intimidate the others. Althea Gibson had also
been a lot like that when she played. She scared all the girls.

Nevertheless, as graceful as Maria was, as overpowering a
personality, as natural a champion, as far as tennis was

concerned I never thought she knew what was going on out there. She was a con, really, because it would have been blasphemy for anybody ever to suggest that someone who looked so good might be lacking.

But in truth, Maria was pretty slow. As graceful as she appeared, she was somewhat knock-kneed, walked like a duck, while the best athletes are often those whose feet point the other way—pigeon-toed. But who noticed with Maria? She had those long, flowing strokes—beautiful textbook shots. She looked like the pictures of Suzanne Lenglen, which were so gorgeous and striking, but which always made me wonder how Lenglen or anybody else had the time to get in such elongated poses. But of course you were picky to ask such rude questions in the face of such grace.

Still, Maria's problem was simply that she wasn't quick enough. When she moved in to volley off her great first serve, she seldom could get much past the service line, but opponents were so taken in by the whole act that they popped high returns back that Maria, as graceful as ever, gracefully put away. Actually, men can often get away with that routine. A man is strong enough so that he can compensate for his slow movement by bulling shots. Women can't do that as often. We must depend much more on technique. The average player—male or female—is always better off studying the women pros.

So, anyway, against Bueno I chipped her low volleys all afternoon, and she was worn down by the third set, which I won 6–1. My first Wimbledon! And when I went back to old toiletless Room 33 at the Lexham, there on my bed was my total prize for winning the championship of the world: six Mars bars that Rosie and some of my other Wightman Cup teammates had bought for me.

Whatever, life sure was less complicated then.

My last years on the road, I seldom left my hotel room except to play, or maybe to sneak out to a movie. This wasn't just because of all the hassle I would get in public. For one thing, I just about lived in ice bags, packing them on both knees—and you'd be amazed how much that lowers your body temperature. Often, I'd be too cold to go out. Also, I simply enjoy my privacy more—reading, TV or music, whatever I choose. As long as a hotel is clean, with a TV and a double bed, I'm happy. Hotels are never very good with laundry, so it helps to be near a Laundromat—but that means going out, and when you meet people, all they want to talk about is tennis. Of course, I would read the sports pages every day, but I don't possess that deep, abiding interest and knowledge of sports that most people assume I do.

I do love just about all kinds of music, though. I'm a WASP who loves the Latin sound, although I have no idea why, and I've also come to enjoy classical music, even if I don't understand it. I like rock—especially from the sixties—and soul, and like a lot of tennis players, my fantasy is to be a rock star. I think I was one of the first players to practice to music. Tennis is more spontaneous, because you never know what's going to happen in a match, but music is self-expression, too; a racket, your voice, or a musical instrument—it's all about the same.

I am most drawn to the dance, though. I saw *The Turning Point*, the movie about ballet, twelve times, which is my record. I think tennis players and other athletes could learn a great deal more about balance by studying dance. I've noticed how dancers always manage to keep the knee directly above the foot, and I think if we better understood those principles of torque, athletes wouldn't have so many knee injuries.

Whatever, I do appreciate that there is some (too much?) spirit of the artist within me, which sounds fancy, but which is probably just counterproductive. Chris, for example, thinks of herself as all science and no art, and now Tracy is the same way. I know that a lot of tennis fans, especially the Europeans, get so irritated when they see all of the two-handed backhand "clones" who have succeeded Chris, and I try to explain that they have had strong, personal coaching virtually since they were babies, plus the well-defined example of Chris to follow, and that possibly they just haven't been required to think for themselves yet. Ultimately, in at least some of these young players, we may see a measure of art tinting the science and mechanics. I was amazed, for example, the first time I met Andrea Leand—not only that she was so bright, but that she could apply what someone older suggested.

When I was younger, my own problem was more the reverse of what these young girls exhibit. For a long time, I would rather hit a beautiful shot instead of a winning one. Spin! I just love it. Spin is such art. It amazes me, looking back, that as driven as I always was, so goal-oriented, that nonetheless I still had to battle my artistic side. So that must run deep within me.

But at last I am a hardheaded pragmatist. I'm suspicious of those who profess to be idealists, and I make sure to check my purse whenever I hear anyone invoke the word "sacrifice"— for the older I grow, the more I perceive that people only sacrifice what they wanted to get rid of all along. What I've seen, wherever in the world, is that nothing works unless self-interest is prominent, if indeed not utterly paramount. Those people I've met who are the most idealistic—and sincerely so—almost invariably turn out to be socialistic, because socialism works out so dandy on paper. Unfortunately, human nature being what it is, I never see any evidence, anywhere, of socialism working off paper, in life. I think being an athlete reinforces your practical side. When your business is to win or lose, and it is just you out there and the result will be marked very clearly on a scoreboard, then I believe you tend naturally to view the world in terms less fuzzy. Anyway, that has been my experience.

The people I just adore are the Italians. So they like to pinch bottoms. They have such wonderful expressions, such a marvelous eye. Italy is about the only place in the world where I really like to shop. Mostly, I just want to go into a store, buy exactly what I need, and get out. I can literally go years without buying new dress-up clothes. But in Italy I can be a regular window-shopper. And it's like what Virginia Ruzici told me someone had pointed out to her: if it wasn't for the Italians designing tennis clothes, we'd all be playing naked.

But the people I feel closest to nowadays are the Japanese. I can sense that they like me, too, and it must be the real thing because usually they prefer women to be blond and cute and well built, and that sure isn't me. I know there is something we share. Wherever I've traveled in the world, I've come to feel recently that the main problem is that people simply don't feel that they're effective anymore, and so there is a growing lack of pride. Or maybe it developed the other way around, with pride going first, and then, because of that, a sense of powerlessness developed.

Anyway, I feel these sad vibrations almost everywhere but in Japan. I have a hypothesis, the Billie Jean King Theory of Room Service, that the way a nation provides room service is the window on its soul. The Japanese are far and away the most effective. The extra effort is always there. It kills me the way a lot of the players take the Japanese to the cleaners and never give them anything back. They know they've got the Japanese over a barrel: the country is a long way from everywhere, but it is rich, so it will pay through the nose for tennis. But the Japanese are coming along. Someday soon they're going to produce a world champion, male or female, and I'm really rooting for that.

I even felt more at peace playing in Japan in the last few years. I didn't play any better there, because then you would be talking about magic. I'm just talking about being comfortable. I actually argued less in Japan. That's the one place I play where I have peace of mind.

10 BIG POINTS

I think that most people have it all wrong about what makes a champion. You read all that about how So-and-So wants to win so much that he would run over his grandmother or beat a little boy at checkers, and that doesn't mean much because everybody would rather win than lose, and it is no trick to beat grandmothers and little boys at just about anything.

The trick is to beat somebody who is just about as good as you. The rest of it is for show.

I only care to win where it matters. I remember playing golf against another player one day, and I shot 94, and I was very happy with that because I was within myself. And my opponent said she made 84, which she did if you didn't count all the mulligans and teeing it up in the fairway and all that—which was fine, too, as far as I was concerned. I didn't care if she carried the ball up to every hole and dropped it in and gave herself an 18. Most times, like that day, I just want to battle me. And if it made the other player happy that she beat me by ten strokes her way, good for her.

In fact, as I said earlier, I detest confrontations. I don't even enjoy cards or games like that. I'll do anything to avoid scenes. Maybe that's why I've had so much success at tennis—because, in effect, I've channeled all my competitive energies into that one place.

The main thing is not a matter of wanting to win; the main thing is being scared to lose. A great many more top tennis players—or outstanding athletes in all sports—have a genuine fear of winning, of finishing it off. I'm quite serious. For the vast majority of players, it is much easier facing a match point against you than trying to finish the other player off.

The match that made Chrissie was the second round of her first U.S. Open, 1971, when she was facing Mary Ann Eisel, who was a ranked player at that time, and Mary Ann had six match points, and she served each one to Chris's backhand at the same pace, and Chris blasted her way out, and when she finally got a match point, she knocked it off. Now, you can say that Mary Ann was stupid to keep hitting the same shot over and over—even if it was her best shot. To myself at the time, I said, Mary Ann, you deserve to lose. But what was even more evident was that Chris was afraid to lose. She was sixteen, but I could see that, and that fascinated me.

But what about the opposite of going all out to win—tanking. Is that really conceivable? Would anyone struggle to get to the very apex and then throw it away? Well, tanking happens a lot more than it is supposed. And I'm not just talking about throwing a Tuesday-night doubles match because you lost the singles that afternoon and want to get out of town. I'm talking about *tanking*—purposely losing the very big ones.

When I was a kid I would never even think about such a thing. It was only after my first knee operation that I ever even considered the possibility. Operations are so frustrating.

First of all, the pain and fear builds up for a year before you finally agree to endure the operation. Then there is a substantial period of recuperation; and then, worst of all, when you come back to play, it always takes longer to regain your form than you ever imagined. And even then, you never come back all the way. Suddenly you decide that you really aren't going to be able to do something anymore, but you won't quite let yourself accept that reality, so you lose on purpose instead. You protect yourself a little longer. Tanking is never just a simple matter of giving up.

It's wonderful in a team sport because you can still go through the motions but refuse to commit yourself. Billy Cunningham, the coach of the Philadelphia 76ers, told me once that when it came down to the wire in a tight game and there was a time-out, you'd be amazed how many great former All-Americans suddenly had to tie their shoes. They didn't want to look at the coach; they didn't want the coach to look at them and think of them; they didn't want the ball. It was very few players, Billy told me, who *wanted* the ball when it really counted.

But in an individual sport you can't hide behind the fact that someone else will carry the load. If you tank, you know you tank. But it can still be a very useful device—and because of that, it can become a habit. Primarily, you see, if you tank you lose, but you don't lose legitimately. Then you can tell yourself that you didn't truly get beaten, since you didn't try. It's a great cop-out.

Sometimes, too, tanking is a way of being masochistic. If you are an athlete, you want to win, so how painful it is to punish yourself by denying yourself victory.

Or, you tank to hurt someone else. I can remember, for example, during the second year of the Virginia Slims tour, when I was angry at Larry about something, totally frustrated, and even though I was playing in the—get this—Billie Jean King Invitational—also get this—which he had con-

ceived, named, and promoted, I showed him how mad I was
at him by throwing a match, and then later throwing a fit,
screaming "You don't care!" at the top of my lungs at Larry,
and then driving off into the night.

I do think that taught me one lesson, which was to avoid
playing in tournaments that Larry promoted. But it did not
altogether cure me of tanking. You may be shocked and I
won't name the match, because I don't want to deprive my
opponent of anything, but *I* absolutely tanked the final of a
Grand Slam tournament once.

Honestly—I threw the match completely. I was in a bad
humor. Larry and I had had a horrible argument that morning. Now you mustn't think that I tank a match every time
Larry and I argue. Even this time, it wasn't so much that we
fought or even what we fought about—which I don't remember—so much as it was that I had to break off the argument
before we finished, because I had to get to the tournament
and dress for the final. The result was that I took the court
with a terrible feeling of incompleteness, which made it all
the harder for me to concentrate on the match. I remember
distinctly, for example, that all of a sudden, in the middle of
the match, my mind started to wander to the state of the
world. Since the state of the world is rarely very good, and
certainly wasn't on this occasion, I became even more depressed and lost more concentration.

Then I decided that the fans didn't like me, that they
weren't fair. All of a sudden, I just said to myself: All right,
people, you can have it. You don't want me to win, and I don't
care all that much about tennis anyway, because I'm angry at
Larry and the world stinks, so to hell with it, people, I'll just
let my opponent have it. And I packed it in at that moment as
sure as if I had picked up my rackets and left the court.

So you can see, I can be such a horrible baby. I know. No
arguments. What I did was inexcusable. I think that someplace where I went wrong was that I was never specific

enough in my goals. Growing up, I only wanted to be "the best." I think if tennis had a lot of well-known records, as they do in our other American sports—baseball, especially—then I would have had more definite targets to shoot for. But I never had a scheme. I'm sure that if I had ever thought about Helen Wills Moody's record of eight Wimbledons, then I could have used that to override some of the distractions I suffered there. But that never crossed my mind. The trouble with me was that I never knew what I had accomplished until years later, when tennis journalist and sports commentator Bud Collins would fill me in on what exactly I had done.

Generally, too—and this will also come as a surprise to most people—I am not, shall we say, "naturally" tough. Day in and day out, I require a great deal of mental preparation. Now this may be good in one sense, because when I am able to get myself up, I can really peak. But there also must be some deep valleys, too.

I think, of all the times I won anything of consequence, the one victory I *willed*, if that is possible, was my last Wimbledon title, in 1975, when I had decided that it would be my swan song from singles. Why, I started to win that months before. That spring, we were playing in a tournament at Lakeway, near Austin, Texas, and I really got robbed on some line calls in one match, and after I got beat, I came into the locker room and I actually threw my racket clear across the place, and I screamed out, "That's it! I'm going to win Wimbledon this year! It's mine!" Real inspirational Knute Rockne coaching stuff. Who was I kidding? Lakeway, Texas, had absolutely nothing to do with Wimbledon.

But this was one occasion when I could get a real fix on things. I worked with weights. I worked out more than ever. I was playing World Team Tennis that summer, and one of my teammates on the New York Apples was Sandy Mayer, who is not only the most textbook-oriented of all players—his father is a coach—but one American male who actually enjoys hitting with females. Sandy worked me day after day. I was so fit when I got over there. And then—wouldn't you know it?—as soon as I got to England I came down sicker than ever, and suddenly it was the semis and I couldn't breathe and Chrissie had me down 0–3, 15–40, in the third. And I said, Hey, Billie Jean, this is ridiculous. You paid the price. For once, you looked ahead. You're supposed to win. Get your bahoola in gear.

And I did. I won six straight games. And two days later I knocked off Evonne, love and one, which was the worst beating in sixty-four years of finals. I really zoned that day.

But of course, there is always another side to the story, which is that you are not exactly playing by yourself out there. You will hear that the reason I cleaned up the court with Chrissie in the '75 semis from down 0–3 in the third had nothing whatsoever to do with me. No, it was all because Chrissie fell apart because she looked up in the stands and saw Jimmy Connors come in, escorting Susan George, the movie star. Well, I never saw Susan George. But then, I wasn't looking for Jimmy Connors. I just had my eyes on destiny. Choose what you want to believe.

It is also true that being primed and being serene doesn't necessarily mean anything. Some players work best when they're mad or unhappy. The worst thing is to expect the same reactions from all the best players. A classic case that nearly destroyed me: Maureen Connolly.

Little Mo. First female Grand Slammer. Great champion. Might have been the best of all if she hadn't been injured in a horseback-riding accident. Tough, high-strung, outgoing, a student of Teach Tennant, who also taught Alice Marble and Bobby Riggs. The plot thickens. And Teach was really some tough cookie.

Now, when I was fifteen years old, on the Junior Wightman Cup Team, Maureen came to help us practice one day, where we were training, on Long Island. That night she singled me out and took me to dinner, and I was so excited, and then, flat-out, she told me, "Look, I just want to let you know: you'll never make it. So don't bother." She almost screamed it at me. Obviously, I was completely crestfallen.

Okay, jump ahead seven years later, to 1966. I was in the locker room at Wimbledon after winning my first title, and Maureen came in and congratulated me. I wanted to take her aside and ask her to replay that evening on Long Island, but there were too many people around and, as I've said, I'm not crazy about personal confrontations. So, I let it pass, and I never saw her again, and three years later—during Wimbledon, in fact—Maureen died of cancer.

I assumed that would be the end of that Long Island episode, but a few years later, a man whose first name is Brent (I forget his last name) came up to me and told me that he had been helping coach the Junior Wightman Cup Team that day Maureen came by. And she watched for a while, and then she asked him who he thought the top prospect was. And, Brent told me, he had answered Maureen by saying Tory Fretz.

Well, he told me, Maureen had only laughed at him when he said that, and then she had pointed over to where I was hitting, and she had said, "Oh no, the only one with any real chance at all is that one."

So the whole business with the dinner and putting me down was Maureen's idea of reverse psychology. She thought that anybody who was going to be a champion needed more spunk, of the sort that Teach Tennant had instilled in her. Only all it did was scare me, because I just wasn't built that way. Maureen was really playing with fire.

You see, ultimately all the psychological mumbo-jumbo counts for nothing if you can't make the shot. I've seen terrific champion-types out there who are just too limited. Nobody has more guts than Kathy Jordan, but that can't compensate enough for her form. Harold Solomon has heart second to none, but even on his favorite surfaces he can't stand up to the strongest players.

The difference between me at my peak and me in the last few years of my career is that when I was the champion I had the ultimate in confidence. When I decided, under pressure, in the tenth of a second, that I had to go with my very weakest shot—forehand down the line—I was positive that I could pull it off. Later, it was different. I still might get by. I might lob my way out or go crosscourt and put off the crunch, make the other player hit another shot. But that's not the same. When I was a champion, I could make myself hit that shot when it mattered the most. Even more than that; going into a match, I knew it was my weakest shot, and I knew in a tight spot my opponent was going to dare me to hit it, and I knew I could hit it those two or three or four times in a match when I absolutely had to. That is a champion.

The cliché is to say that the champions play the big points better. Yes, but that's only the half of it. The champions play their weaknesses better—because the odds are that you'll get your weakness thrown at you on a big point.

And it certainly helped that I thrived on big points. In fact, I've never understood players who didn't. That was what I dreamed about as a kid—not somebody giving Billie Jean her ninth Wimbledon plate, but Billie Jean serving for the final, but down 30–40, second serve. Hey, that's what it's all about for me. That's like running barefoot through the forest.

I've heard about Pete Rose at the 1980 World Series, where some of the other players—the younger players—could not understand his exuberance. He was running around like a little boy, and he couldn't stop talking about the experience. And Rose had been in World Series before. But it was obvious that the more chaos, the more attention, the better he liked it. "Hey," he said, "of course I like it. This is what I play for." Me, too. Whenever I would feel the pressure because I was in some major final, I would tell myself, Wait, Billie Jean, this is what you've been aiming for. All your life. Why, Randy and I used to sit at the dining-room table, practicing our autographs for that time when we were grown up and people would ask for our autographs. I put a great deal of thought into how I would make my *M*'s. I tried this way and that, over and over.

Of all the stands I've taken in tennis, I'm sure, looking back, that one thing I'm proudest of is the fact that when the tiebreaker came into tennis I was one of the very few players—male or female—who wanted it. And, for that matter, I still think tournament tennis would be better off with the sudden-death tiebreaker that we use in Team Tennis: nine points, first one to reach five wins. Tennis is already too much a game of second chances. People say tiebreakers are short enough and therefore the chance of luck or a hot streak deciding a set are too great unless you have to win by two points. And yes, that's true. But tennis is a game, and it is entertainment and sometimes concessions must be made to that fact. Sometimes an athlete simply must face the music. Sometimes a whole career can turn on just a few points.

Larry and I were watching on television when Borg and McEnroe played the final of the U.S. Open in 1980. Borg, remember, had beaten McEnroe in that great five-setter a couple months before, to win his fifth straight Wimbledon. There was an aura about him now, the same sort of feeling that existed about Connors before Ashe beat him at Wimbledon in 1975. And then Borg lost the first set to McEnroe. And the way he lost it: not once, but twice he served for the set. And both times he failed.

After the second time, I turned to Larry and I said, "It's over. He's never going to be the same again."

Larry said, "You're saying Borg will never win again?"

"No, I didn't say that. He's much too good for that. He might possibly even come back and win today. But what I said was that he'll never be the same again. The bubble has burst, and he knows that himself."

I could see it in Borg's eyes in the close-ups. His armor was pierced, and soon McEnroe would understand that, too. With every champion there are moments that build your career and there are those that tear it down. Until September 7, 1980, Borg had been riding a tiger. But he fell off that day.

The horrible part is, too, that a lot of us never enjoy it when we are at the top. Maybe Borg did. The players today have so much done for them that they can stop occasionally and smell the roses. But I know I didn't have the opportunity to savor what I had accomplished, and I imagine that is the way it is with most champions.

The trouble with being number one in the world—at anything—is that it takes a certain mentality to attain that position in the first place, and that is something of a driving, perfectionist attitude, so that once you do achieve number one, you don't relax and enjoy it. I remember, after I won my first Wimbledon, and we were driving to Wales the next day, and I was so sick, that Gerry Williams, the British writer who was with Larry and me, said, "Why are you doing this?" And I just said, "But Gerry, now I have to prove myself." I had to show that my winning Wimbledon was no fluke. Winning Wimbledon drove me even more. Once you become number one, your main thought is to protect that, to get better still, to stay ahead of number two. It's unfortunate, but almost by definition, if you are the best, if you are the champion of the world, you can't take much pleasure in it—or otherwise you couldn't be the best.

(Left) My mother and father.
(Above) Mom and I when I was a year old and Dad was off at war.
Courtesy Betty, Bill, and Randy Moffitt

(Right) I was five years old at the time this was taken, brother Randy being three months.
Courtesy Betty, Bill, and Randy Moffitt

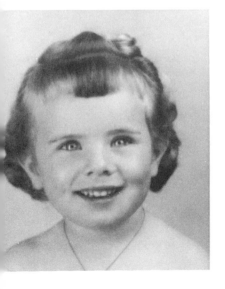

(Left) In the front yard, with Dad.
(Below left) In my high school graduation gown.
(Below right) The defensive back going after Randy was twelve at the time.
Courtesy Betty, Bill, and Randy Moffitt

(Left) We were married on
September 9, 1965.
Courtesy UPI
(Below) The baby in
the middle is Lucy.
*Courtesy Betty, Bill,
and Randy Moffitt*

(Below) Perhaps the only peaceful moment I ever had at
Wimbledon. It was 1973, and I won the triple—singles, doubles,
and mixed. *Courtesy Wide World Photos*

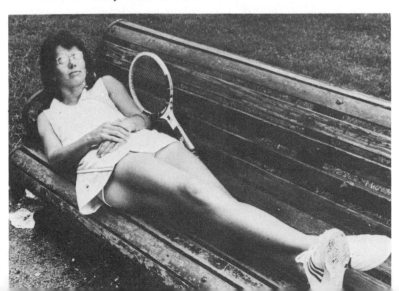

(Above) My final with Chris was postponed a day by rains that year. *Courtesy Wide World Photos*
(Right) The face is familiar. *Courtesy Jerry Cooke, Sports Illustrated*
(Below) The Conquering Heroine arrives! *Courtesy Wide World Photos*

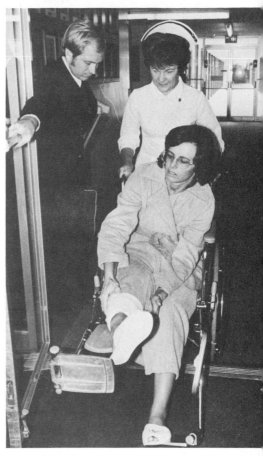

(*Above*) Rosie and I
had just lost the match—1975.
Courtesy Wide World Photos
(*Right*) November of 1976, and I'm
returning home after knee surgery.
Courtesy Wide World Photos
(*Below*) With my special mentor
and early coach, Alice Marble,
at the Colgate Inaugural
in Palm Springs, 1976.
Courtesy Dina Makarova

(*Above*) An old-fashioned low five for Chris, while the other 1977 Wightman Cup members watch: (*from left*) JoAnne Russell, Kristien Kemmer Shaw, Rosie Casals. *Courtesy Cheryl A. Traendly*
(*Below*) Up on stage with Elton John and ready to sing backup at his 1977 Madison Square Garden concert. *Courtesy Dina Makarova*

(Left) And a dancer's form: Wimbledon, 1972. *Courtesy Tony Triolo,* Sports Illustrated *(Below)* This is a fantasy come true—me, in 1978, flanked by Cynthia Gregory and Rudolph Nureyev. *Courtesy Wide World Photos*

(Above left) The Wimbledon plate and a curly-haired victor.
Courtesy Tony Triolo, Sports Illustrated
(Above right) Speaking to you from high above Centre Court . . .
Courtesy Melinda Phillips
(Below) Martina and I have just accepted the doubles trophy from
the Duchess of Kent in 1979. This was my record twentieth
Wimbledon title. *Courtesy Wide World Photos*

(Above) At the press conference when I acknowledged my relationship with Marilyn Barnett. *Courtesy Cheryl A. Traendly*
(Below) Larry and I at the trial last December: behind us, Marilyn returning to her seat. *Courtesy Jim McHugh/PEOPLE Weekly/© 1981 Time Inc.*

II WOULDJA, COULDJA, CANYA?

People say I'm crazy, doing what I'm doing
Well, they give me all kind of warnings to save me from ruin
When I say that I'm OK they look at me kind of strange
Surely you're not happy now you no longer play the game
　　　　　　　—John Lennon, "Watching the Wheels"

If you cannot truly enjoy being a champion, then, as I discovered, it is even more difficult being famous these days. Now, I'm not wearing a hair shirt, I'm not saying that I don't like being noticed and appreciated, and I certainly understand that fame can translate into money, but it is also true that fame can rob you of a great deal. Unless you want to lock yourself in a room all day long—which is often exactly what I do when I'm traveling—someone whose face is well known is simply not able any longer to function in a normal manner in the everyday world. The main problem with being a celebrity is that there are simply so many interruptions all the time that you are never able to complete a simple thought process in one sitting. Everything is stop-and-go. I always feel that timing is off, that somehow I'm incomplete.

Also taken from you is the natural right to be an observer. I can rarely people-watch. I can only be the one examined.

Unquestionably, too, I'm sure it's worse being a female celebrity because with us there is always such an inordinate amount of interest in our sex lives. It took me a while to understand, but as much as I hated the press for asking all those nontennis questions, I finally appreciated that they weren't sexist. Not really, not in the usual sense. No, they were just plain interested in sex. You take the average man, and present him with an average woman, and the average subject is going to be sex—not finance or the oil crisis or tennis. As much as I might not like that, I'm afraid that's normal, not sexist.

You know who seemed to understand that instinctively, and at a very early age? Chrissie. Little Miss American Pie. She was always adept at playing the role of the vulnerable little lady, but inserting sex into a press conference in a very coy way. I have to give her credit the way she has always led those press guys on. And then, too, I have to give the tennis press credit for improving so over the years, for more and more switching the emphasis from sex to tennis.

I am a realist, and from a strictly pragmatic point of view, it's probably just as well that the sporting press is so predominantly male and that they did ask so many wrong, irrelevant questions down through the years. To be perfectly honest, given the total attendance that tennis attracts and the television ratings that it racks up, we have, through the years, gotten more coverage than we fairly have warranted. And I'm not so sure but that one of the reasons why this is so is because the male sportswriters have been attracted to tennis as a whole because of the sex angle, because of the female players.

As a matter of fact, one of the reasons why I never enjoyed my personal publicity as much as I should have is because I always felt a little guilty that I was receiving attention that went well beyond what *any* tennis player properly deserved. I've simply never been satisfied that tennis has ever become major league. I think that's why it was always so easy for me to identify so with Wimbledon, because that is the one place where the interest and coverage of tennis reached the levels that I always associated with baseball and football.

Of course, in the beginning the last thing I ever complained about was too much fame. The first time I saw any real headlines in America for women's tennis was in Chicago, in the *Tribune*, at that Wightman Cup in 1961, the time when Karen was running off with Rod Susman. I was so excited about the publicity that I was calling up my folks and reading them the headlines long-distance. But that was an aberration. All through the sixties we got only the tiniest coverage. Most times I couldn't even find the results of major tournaments in the largest and best American newspapers. And on TV— forget it. The breakthrough didn't come until 1971, when, in a very short period of time, Chrissie made her big smash at Forest Hills and then I went over the $100,000 mark in purse money for a year. Those two things together changed every-thing—and largely for the wrong reasons, of course.

The dollar part is especially ironic, because money has never meant that much to me, but I thought it was crucial for the acceptance and integrity of women's tennis that one of us make six figures, and since I was the only one with a shot at it, I absolutely wore myself out in the chase. I won nineteen tournaments that year. Nowadays it is the rare star, male or female, who even plays nineteen tournaments a year. I finally went over the $100,000 goal by beating Wendy Overton in the quarters at Phoenix in October, but we counted everything in that total—a car I had won and other merchandise. I ended up with $117,000, though, so it was an honest achievement. It really did impress the fans and the media, too.

It makes me laugh today when I read about "all-time money winners" in tennis—or any sport. Inflation and the greater purses have made any historical financial comparisons in sports meaningless. The most prize money I ever made was in 1980, my last full year on the circuit, when I picked up $298,000 in less than six months. Players' earnings are never so much as they seem, either. Athletes have such a brief period in the real big money and, especially for those in an individual sport, expenses can be killing. Living quite modestly, a tennis player on tour would still have to put out a minimum of $30,000 to travel for a year.

Still, it is important for any sport to hype its money figures. If you don't make a big deal these days out of the fact that somebody's going to win $40,000 in a tournament, then most fans will decide that it can't be a very important tournament. Money talks.

Naturally, everyone assumes that I made a fortune against Bobby Riggs, but the grand total, tops, from all sources, was no more than $150,000. A small amount of that was for a brief appearance I made on the TV show *The Odd Couple*, where the script called for Bobby and me to play table tennis against each other. It's been almost a decade, but reruns of that show still pop up regularly and, I swear, it's not uncommon for kids who were too young to appreciate the actual match in the Astrodome to come up to me and say, "Hey, I saw you on *The Odd Couple.*" That's good, I guess. It reminds me that there's a whole big world out there that never cared for a moment about tennis.

Bobby tried to talk me into a rematch—tennis, not table tennis—and he assured me that I could get a guaranteed minimum of a million dollars, with the possibility of doubling that. I believed him completely, too. Bobby may shoot his mouth off for a lot of publicity reasons, but the one thing he never kidded about was money. But never mind; there wasn't enough money in the world to make me play him again, to go through all that. He still keeps asking, though. Bobby never quits. I love him. I think he's hysterical.

I don't have nearly as much money as a lot of the kids today who haven't won anywhere near the championships I did. Part of it is that I never made as much as people imagine, and part of it is that I lost a lot of projects that I believed in— *womenSports* magazine, World Team Tennis, the smokeless ashtray Larry invented. But it was worth it. Those things mattered to us. The only bad part about my not having much money is that people think I do and expect me to carry on like an empress.

As I said, Chrissie's coming on the scene was important, too, and not only for women's tennis, but for me, personally, because it gave the press a duel to play up. That's why the men have been so lucky recently, first with Borg–Connors, then with Borg–McEnroe, because in both instances the two rivals were not only competitive opponents but distinctly different personality types. In fact, as I've mentioned already, Chris and I aren't all that much different as people, but we are perceived to be opposites, and our style surely is, so the press could offer us up as a real rivalry.

Today, whereas Chris and Tracy are quite different as individuals, they play the same game, appear to be the same types, and thus provide no raw material for the press to build them up as rivals. Martina hasn't been much help, either. Americans are never much attracted to foreign players *on their own.* At her peak as a Czechoslovakian, Martina didn't draw well, and Borg has never been the box-office draw in the U.S. that he's been in Europe. But a foreigner takes on real gloss if he or she is a foil, the other part of the act. Borg *with* Connors or McEnroe is a sale. Hana *with* Tracy or Chris could turn out to be the same thing. (Martina, of course, is such a more complicated piece of business, and it's impossible to guess right now what the reaction to her as a U.S. citizen will be in the next few years. If the warm reception at the 1981 Open was any fair indication, she will only get more popular.)

Anyway, the unfortunate—for me—aspect of Chris's arrival on the scene was that it encouraged the press to stereotype me all the more. Even before Chris, I was already pretty well labeled, too. In the beginning it was so hard for me to understand, but that no matter how reasonable I tried to sound, no matter how cool and pragmatic and MOR, I always was portrayed as a radical.

It is very hard to be a female leader. While it is assumed that any man, no matter how tough, has a soft side—in fact, a lot of male writers go out of their way to find a springtime in every Hitler—any female leader is assumed to be one-dimensional. The fact that I wasn't supposed to possess any gentleness, that hurt me the most of all. You bet it hurt. I would cry to myself about that. But I've never been very good about letting my feelings show when I'm wounded. Under those circumstances, my body language covers up with a smile, and that probably assured a lot of people that I really was the callous shrew that I was made out to be.

Of course, if I had been a young guy with the exact same desires and feelings that were always attributed to me, then things would have been altogether different. Then I not only would have been a star; I would have been a hero as well— right? The endorsements would have poured in. It's always easier to be a man fighting for something.

I did try, too. Often, at the start of press conferences, I would go out of my way to urge—nicely—that none of us should be too dogmatic, that there were different shadings to the meanings for relatively new expressions like "women's lib" and "feminist." But nobody was listening; it never made any difference. Whenever the word "feminist" was applied to me, I could tell, it was used pejoratively.

I think it helped the press to make up its mind about me quickly, too, because of my playing style. A real female-feminine-lady player is supposed to have a certain kind of nonsweaty lady's manner, and I was the worst of both worlds. I not only had an aggressive, net-rushing style, but I didn't look that part, the way someone stylishly long-legged like Bueno did. I had to grub it out on the court. So I was never described in ways that related to the female gender. No code words like "cute" or "elegant" were ever dragged up for Billie Jean. And the classic example: I always wore lots of jewelry on court. I mean, anybody could see that. But nobody in the press ever wrote about the jewelry I had on, because that contradicted the tough-broad image they had decided on. But as soon as Chris began playing, if she so much as had earrings on, that was sure to be mentioned in everybody's story. That's how the press pegs you.

A mistake I made was that I should have employed a public-relations agent years before I finally did. When at last I decided that I would hire one, and Pat Kingsley in Los Angeles was suggested, she didn't want the account because she didn't want to handle a "tough bitch." That's how bad my PR was, that a PR expert didn't think PR could salvage me. Pat, like so many people who finally meet me, was amazed to discover how physically small I am, how well-behaved, how ladylike. In fact, at parties, I have actually had people come *back* over to me at the end of the evening and tell me a second time, "I still can't believe that this is you." Apparently, they had such a negative preconception of me that after they met me at the beginning of the party, they were so shocked at my demeanor that they figured I must be putting on for a moment, so they kept an eye on me the rest of the time, checking me out.

Too often it has seemed to me that the press can be narrow-minded, lacking vision. Anybody with a new idea is immediately portrayed as a huckster—instead of as a pioneer, perhaps; as someone with imagination. The New York press is the worst because it takes itself too seriously. I don't think it's any surprise that World Team Tennis was accepted so much faster in the western part of the U.S., because the press out there is more open-minded and not disposed to immediately knock anything new.

The press also has its favorite little formula in all sports, which I could never understand: preferring r/u's to win. Well, I came to understand: it makes a better story, and never mind anything else. If a winner keeps winning, what new is there to say? If you're going to win, you better win big and you better never stop winning. That way, the press can start calling you a dynasty if you are a team or say you may be the all-time best if you are an individual. It always bugged me that the press would make a bigger fuss over someone like Virginia Wade or Arthur Ashe for winning an occasional big title than it did over Chris Evert or Rod Laver, who won championships every year.

It's more understandable to me—but still irritating—that the press keeps confusing competition with quality. For best example: everybody still makes a big fuss over the "great" Wimbledon final I played with Margaret in 1970, when I led in both sets, but lost 14–12, 11–9. What a classic! Oh yeah; if either one of us had played up to our average form, the other would have been lucky to take a couple of games. But as it was, we were both lucky to be on our feet. Margaret had her injured ankle shot full of novocaine just before we came out, and my knee was so bad I had to have it operated on the very next week. I don't think I could manage to get to the net more than a couple times in the whole dreary forty-six games. But in the press, it was, and will forever remain, a great all-time match.

It's especially funny, too, because one day a few years ago, when there was rain at Wimbledon, a tape of that match was broadcast during the delay. And, very tentatively, Chris came up to me afterward, and she told me she'd seen the match, and then she dared to ask me, "Was it really any good?"

"Are you kidding?" I said. "It was terrible."

"Oh, I'm so glad to hear you say that," Chris said, "because I'd heard all these great things about that match, and I thought it stunk."

It also is a continual irritation to me how little the sports press knows about sports business. It must learn more about what surrounds a tournament, and not just the games and the personalities that comprise one. In many ways I agree with Dick Butera, Julie Anthony's husband, my boss when he owned the Philadelphia Freedoms of WTT, who says that our constitutional framers made the mistake of leaving out one word in the First Amendment; it should be: "freedom of the *responsible* press."

But the trouble with me is, I like to talk, and I have always enjoyed talking to the press because I like many journalists personally. And I'll say this (I'll shout it from the rooftops): that whatever our differences, I know that the press and I had good mutual instincts. And I'll never forget that when it mattered the very most, they came through for me.

When I had my press conference to disclose my relationship with Marilyn, the press was so thoughtful of my feelings. When I said those words *I had an affair with Marilyn Barnett,* I could hear so many of them in the room actually suck in their breath, and at the end there were so many of them who called out "Good luck" to me. You think that didn't mean a lot to me? Pat Kingsley is much more used to dealing with the show-biz press than the sports press, but she knows how tough sportswriters can be, and she told me later how utterly flabbergasted she was at the decent, gentle manner which so much of the press displayed toward me.

And, of course, virtually all of them were men. You do get a few female tokens on the sports pages now (they're easy to spot at the newspaper office: the female sportswriter is at her desk right where a visitor comes in, next to the one black sportswriter), but I've had to speak almost exclusively to men through the years. In fact, I think that the absolute worst speech I ever gave in my life was a few years ago in California when I was asked to address a feminist group. I got to the podium and looked out and it was all *women* down there. I'd never seen so many women in all my life. I completely choked.

It is nice seeing some female sportswriters around now, but the trouble is, they're unique, just as we female athletes used to be, so it's hard for many of the women writers to remain professional with me at all times. You know, they want to tell me all about their problems in the big, bad men's world. It's the worst with flight attendants. They seem to have some compulsion to fawn over me.

But when it comes to anybody using me, in whatever way, I always try to consider the intention. For example, if I'm getting on a plane somewhere and some flight attendant all of a sudden sees me and blurts out, "You're Billie Jean King," I understand how the element of surprise has gotten to her, and I'll just laugh and whisper, "Yeah, I know I am and you know I am, but let's see if we can't keep it a secret from everybody else." And then maybe if I'm lucky I can curl up in my seat under a blanket and breathe and sleep a little.

But if—and this has happened a few times—I do get to sleep, and a flight attendant comes over to me and, with premeditation, wakes me up and asks me for an autograph, then I am not exactly gracious with her. On a few occasions I have had a flight attendant wake me up and explain that the pilot wants my autograph. Can you believe some people?

Of course, you've got to understand that the human race is generally weird on the subject of autographs. A lot of alleged adults think it is their right to barge in and interrupt you at anything and ask for an autograph—especially so long as it is supposed to be for some child. And autographs are epidemic.

Once one person has asked for one, everyone else feels the
right to follow. For example, if I go to a doctor's office, I know
I'm either going to come out of there scot-free, without having
to sign a single autograph, or one patient or nurse will ask for
my signature and then I'll have to sign for everyone in the
place. There's no in-between with autographs.

And, of course, there's never enough. If you sign a hundred
and turn down the hundred and first—hey, you're a selfish,
big-headed bum. And the horrible thing is, I know what
they're thinking, and if I were in their shoes, I'd probably
sympathize with them to some degree. Here's what's on their
mind: "It's a small price of fame to pay. You rich bitch, if I
made the kind of money you're making, I'd be happy to put
up with just a few more autographs."

It's just that nobody out there understands how much of it
there is. It's worse in sports because we're more accessible
than the stars in show business, and I suspect it's worst of all
in an individual sport, like tennis or golf, because you are not
insulated in any way by a team.

The major entertainment celebrity I've been closest to was
Elton John. We felt a certain kinship. We were both at the
height of our careers at that time we met, in '73; we both wear
glasses; and we're both so competitive—you should hear the
names that man calls me when we play tennis. I was a real
Elton groupie for a while. I'd go to his concerts and Elton
would even get me up on the stage as a BV—a backup
vocalist. I loved it. But when a performance was over, I had to
be in his car waiting, because when he came offstage the
guards were going to escort him to that car and then it was
going to fly off. No one in sports ever gets that sort of
insulation.

I also sense that the fans identify more with the individual-
sport athlete because the chances are that they play the sport
themselves. It makes them feel more part of the family: We
both hit backhands, don't we? We both hit six-irons—that

kind of rationale. And since the fan plays tennis or golf for leisure, he or she has trouble remembering that it is a business to us. Someone will sidle up to Arnold Palmer or Janie Blalock in the middle of a round and start chatting with them as if it were a Saturday morning best-ball back at the country club.

I can sense, too, that when I'm alone people will take more liberties with me. Just being with one other person provides me with a certain implicit protection. I would never eat by myself in public. You are really vulnerable then. They really have you pinned down. It's hard enough to get people to leave you alone when you're having dinner with someone. For example, here is a dinner conversation I had not long ago. It is fairly typical; there have been hundreds like this one down through the years; I just happen to recall this one so clearly because it happened recently.

Larry and I are having a quiet meal in a restaurant. Well-dressed man and woman, obviously tipsy, approach.

Man: "Hey, Billie Jean, give me your autograph."

Larry: "Give me your autograph, *please.*"

I don't say a word, but apparently my expression indicates agreement with Larry's remark, because it is to me, then, that the woman turns.

Woman: "Well, aren't you the little bitch."

Larry: "Billie Jean, don't you sign anything."

Woman (pushing a paper at me): "We support you, you know."

I take the paper from the man's hand and scribble my signature, saying, "No, I'll sign for him. He just doesn't have any manners. But I won't sign for you, lady, because you don't own me."

You can't ever win. Surely only a selfish bitch would refuse to donate one of her extra rackets to a worthwhile cause. Only, a hundred worthwhile causes a year asking for a racket apiece equals . . . Plus autographed photographs, clothes, shoes, balls . . . Wouldja, couldja, canya, Billie Jean? Just this one time. Just this one more. The aggravation never stops.

They get you both ways. If you do anything that smacks of the ostentatious, then you're a conceited show-off. People assume that you have let fame go to your head, that you must be an entirely different—and worse—person. I can't tell you how many times old acquaintances, people who barely knew me in school (and didn't really try to know me, either), come up and start the conversation with "Now that you're rich and famous, you're probably . . ."

If, however, you act yourself, if you don't behave in any sort of unusual way, people are also disappointed at that. I'm always being told by strangers how amazed they are that I don't travel with a regular entourage. If I'm not accompanied by a palace guard, then they get irritated: "It's not really you."

"Yes, it is."

"Come on, don't put me on. You can't be Billie Jean King."

I remember once I was driving my cute little Jensen-Healy in Los Angeles, and when I stopped at a red light, the guy who drove up in the lane next to me recognized me, and he started screaming—*screaming*—at me, "What'rya doin' in that piece of junk? You should be in a Rolls."

Then there are the insecure little people who are determined to use me in a way so they can hate both me and themselves all the more. These are usually people I have met once before, maybe eight years ago, at a reception somewhere. So they'll start off the conversation by saying, "Remember me?" And boy, are they masochistically thrilled when you say you're sorry you don't. It just proves what a rotten, self-centered person I am and what a piece of nothing they are. Usually these people have brought a friend along with them, and they nod smugly at the friend when I don't remember them.

It takes a very sophisticated person to understand how

many people someone like me meets in the course of a year, and that when I cannot place someone right away, someone who should be familiar to me, it is no reflection on anything but the normal pressures of memory. If someone will just help me out, put our association in context, I usually can recall them. That is, if they just say something like "Remember, Billie Jean, I was with that group you had dinner with in Boston three years ago, that night you lost to Evonne." Then I'll remember.

Rarest of all are the really secure people. I've probably met David Mitchell, the president of Avon, thirty times, but on each new occasion when he sees me, he'll say something like "Billie Jean, I don't know if you remember me, but I'm David Mitchell of Avon." And, of course, those are the people who you do remember.

I don't mean to be the Emily Post of celebrity protocol, but obviously, no two people who happen to become famous deal with this situation the same way. Chrissie, for example, loves going out and being recognized; she really enjoys being a superstar and all that goes with it; she's afraid she'll go out sometime and *not* be recognized. And while I am a private person—literally claustrophobic in some instances, such as on crowded elevators—I also will acknowledge that there is a part of me that is a natural public figure. As always, Larry seems to understand this best. When my parents were first complaining how we weren't gracing them with any grand-children, Larry told them flat-out, "Look, Billie Jean is meant for something else. She'll give much, much more to all of us than she ever would having a baby."

The worst part of being famous is that, in every way, it is the loudest, the brashest, the rudest people who approach you. If you sign those hundred autographs, it surely is the nicer bunch of kids who are in the second hundred and get squeezed out. And the ones with deals and promises and guarantees are almost certain to be the ones full of bull and full of themselves. One of the reasons that so many people who achieve fame and fortune don't find happiness is because, almost by definition, if you reach that high estate you are going to find yourself surrounded by the lowest hangers-on in the world. It is not that you get cut off from the real people; you just get cut off from the good people. And pretty soon, if you don't watch out, you can start to turn into a creep yourself.

Anyway, sometimes I'll sign my autographs "Happiness always" because I know that's what everyone, myself included, would like to hear.

12 THE GIRL PLAYING LINDA SIEGEL

The trouble with me as a woman, and especially as a very visible woman, someone who is perceived as a leader in women's battles, is that I was brought up as a girl in a boy's world, and an awful lot of attitudes—prejudices—are locked within me. I certainly did not let this information slip out at the time, but a major reason why I had to seclude myself for so long in advance of the match with Bobby Riggs was to help me get comfortable with the idea of beating a man. Even now, that's very hard for me to deal with; some things are deeply ingrained.

My brother ended up as a successful major-league pitcher, and for a few years in there he was one of the best relievers in baseball. I mean, here was a young man achieving a goal that not one kid in ten thousand makes, and yet obviously Randy did not attain the heights that I did, and this was always very troublesome to me. I always worried about Randy's ego vis-à-vis my own success.

To be perfectly honest, to this day I'm not altogether sure that I could have made myself beat Riggs except for the fact that what he stood for—or, at least, what he professed to stand for—began to supersede who he was. If Bobby had been the same player, but just a normal fifty-five-year-old, a nice guy—if he had been, for example, Don Budge or Frankie Parker—I have no confidence whatsoever that I could have worked myself up enough to beat him. I am not supposed to beat men.

You bet I was nervous against Riggs. I think women have more of a fear of the unknown than men do. A good case in point is Renee Richards. When she suddenly appeared on the scene, virtually every player immediately assumed that she had to be Wonder Woman. If they had just taken the trouble to talk to the men who had played her, or had watched Renee play for five minutes, they could have seen right away that although she had a great serve she was slow and had bad eyes—even if she is an ophthalmologist. Maybe because I'd already had one trip into the unknown, against Riggs, I wasn't so troubled about Renee.

It so happened that just about the time Renee was making her move into women's tennis, I was coming back from a knee operation. I was supposed to make my reentry into the Virginia Slims championships as a wild card, but the promoters lost their guts and bumped me. I was returning to shape and needed some match action, so I called up Gladys Heldman, who was holding a little tournament, named the Lionel Cup, featuring Renee. She was stunned when I asked her if she could put me in the draw, because almost all the other players were blackballing Renee. "Look, Gladys," I said, "if the doctors say she's a woman, that's good enough for me. No, I'll go even further. If Renee thinks she's a woman in her heart and mind, then she is a woman."

And then, matter-of-factly, Gladys mentioned that Renee was staying only a few blocks away from me in New York, and so I called her up and went over, and we spent several

hours together, really getting to know each other. And at the
end, she even wrote out a prescription for a little eye problem
I had.

As for Riggs, what worried me most about him also involved sight. The Astrodome has this huge white ceiling, and
looking up there into the lights, *if* you could spot the ball, it
was nearly impossible to gain any depth perception. For
weeks leading up to the match I hit about a hundred and fifty
overheads a day because I knew Bobby would throw lobs at
me all night. And you know something? In the three sets, I
don't think I missed one overhead by more than an inch off
the sweet spot—and I also don't think I saw a single ball,
either.

But make no mistake: I was nervous. A few days before the
match, Teddy Tinling brought my dress over for me to try on.
It was the most glorious creation of his whole career, covered
in this sort of cellophane, but it was just plain itchy, and there
was no way I could risk wearing it. Luckily, Teddy had a
backup, another model, and that was the "original" I wore.
Then, the day before the match, as part of the hype, Larry
played a set against Bobby. And that was really frightening,
because the two men had hit a couple months before and
Larry had thought they were fairly evenly matched, but now,
keeping score, Larry couldn't even take a game from Bobby.
Suddenly this whole aura about Riggs, the quintessential con
man, the guy who never lost a hustle—suddenly that really
began to strike home.

To tell you the truth, I was shaking in my shoes right up
until the crossover after the first game; but then I glanced
over at Bobby and that's where I saw that he was scared, too.
He was hyperventilating, nervous in that different kind of
way. That was the first time I was able to truly believe that he
was only a person, like me; he wasn't just a man.

And it's a funny thing, but once I understood that, and then
once I went on and beat him, it didn't mean anything. It was

only something I had to do. And yet I'm not naive. I know very well how much that victory of mine enhanced my reputation. It gave me a credibility I had never earned properly by winning mere Wimbledons and Forest Hills. And while it didn't thrill me in the least, I know that it was important to others. Women still come up and tell me how their husband had to do the dishes for a month, their boss had to make the coffee—things like that. Bella Abzug probably cleaned up more than anybody. "Do you know how many congress*men* there are?" she asked me once.

But for me, Riggs was certainly not the millennium. As I said, I still carry some outright biases based on sex, and not all of them pro-female. For example, whenever I have the choice at customs, I will always go to a male agent. I don't mean I'm smuggling diamonds and dope; it is just that I believe that women are more inclined to go by the book and turn something into a hassle. Of course, so much of it is socialized training. Women aren't instructed to be logical, to roll with the punches. It's like that old business about a woman's intuition. Well, probably that's right. But it's only because we're trained to look outside ourselves, to understand other people better. It isn't intuitive; it's how we've been guided. I always tend to treat men with more care, because I know they're more ego-directed and thus can be wounded more easily.

I've also noticed that even the most allegedly progressive and enlightened men revert back to ancient form on a personal basis. By that I mean that in the abstract they can be tough and say how modern they are, treating women exactly as they do men, but that breaks down one-to-one. I have never met a man who didn't suddenly grow very protective of us touring women players as soon as he got close to us.

Maybe it's because they see up close how very hard it still is to be a woman in a man's world. I really take little satisfaction in all the "firsts" I have accumulated, because all that really indicates is how far behind most of us still are. Even if we are out there in more numbers all the time, it remains so difficult to fight the battles on men's own battlefields day after day. It is only very recently that men have accepted the fact that there are women athletes out there. Believe me, it was only a decade or so ago, pre-Riggs, when it was common for people to ask us in airports and hotels if we weren't "racket salesgirls."

Part of the problem is that I think most men assume that any woman on the road is bound to be what my father used to call a "roundheels." When I was only seventeen, I was staying with some older friends, a family, and all of a sudden, as we were driving along in the car, the wife and her kid up front, the husband in back with me, he starts trying to sneak a feel off of me. I mean, with his wife up front! What could I say? At seventeen, I figured it must be some kind of mistake. But sure enough, the next day, back at the house, he came into the bedroom where I was staying and really started after me. When I protested, he said, "Aw, come on, don't kid me, Billie Jean. You must be a real woman of the world out on that tennis tour."

The fact is that most of the players never even get the opportunity to be women of the world. One of the younger and more expressive ones was practically screaming at me and Sharon Walsh in the locker room one day. "I'm ready," she hollered. "I'm ready for an affair."

Sharon said, "Gee, you're a real romanticist."

"No, just horny," the kid replied.

It used to be that most of the girls on tour simply had no expectations of meeting a nice boy on tour. That is changing, but still, often when a player has a date it is with somebody from back home or from college. If you know a guy from where you grew up, he is more likely to accept you for being a person, but on the road a man you meet takes you for a freak, a jockette, a roundheels—whatever.

Of course, it's altogether different on the men's tour. You go to any men's tournament, and it's practically a fashion parade of local cuties around the court at all times. No matter if he's not one of the better players, no matter if he's not exactly Prince Charming, a male player has a pretty easy time latching on to something. Boy, what I know about some of the fellows—as somebody said, it would make a great book! Never mind prize money and publicity. When we reach the point where the women athletes are getting their pick of dates just as easily as the men athletes, then we've really and truly arrived. Parity at last!

Of course, I'm being somewhat facetious when I say that. There are still some differences—thank God—between us. I know very well, for example, that most of the boys on tour wouldn't think anything of a one-nighter, but even in these sexually liberated times, girls are really not all that free and easy.

But understand: we're traveling and we're lonely and we do get horny. We're very vulnerable. Once one of the absolutely brightest players on tour fell madly in love with a man she met on the road, and she was actually going to marry him until, at the eleventh hour, her parents discovered that the scoundrel already had a wife.

Another time there was a man associated with tennis who traveled a great deal with the Slims tour on business, and he was double-dealing. He was whispering sweet nothings to both—well, let's just call them Blonde and Brunette. Blonde was really beautiful, and most of us—Blonde included—thought that this guy was really in love with her. Most of us—Blonde included—didn't even know he had anything going with Brunette.

We were playing in Lake Bluff, Illinois, one week, and there was a tournament party one night, with all sorts of guests, because some of these local women were going to play doubles with us the next morning in a pro-am. Blonde and I didn't go to the party, but we were only a few hundred yards away, practicing—and, luckily, out of earshot.

Suddenly, Brunette and Mr. Wonderful stand up and the combo strikes up a *ta-da*, and they take the microphone and announce their engagement. Well, when I heard about it the next morning, I was absolutely flabbergasted. The same older ladies were there, ready for the pro-am to start, and they were fluttering around Brunette, cooing over her ring, and here comes Blonde, sauntering happily along.

As you might expect, I was the elder statesman dispatched to go out and intercept Blonde; and I did, and I told her what had happened, and it was about as hard as anything I ever did. She was so hurt, and so angry, and of course there's nothing right you can say in that sort of situation, so I just summoned up my best win-this-one-for-the-Gipper voice and said, "Okay, Blonde, now you go out there and play like crazy in this pro-am!" That was probably the only time any player anywhere ever got a pep talk for a pro-am.

And just for the record, Brunette later broke up with the two-timer, and she and Blonde married other men. In fact, Blonde has married a couple of other men.

If we don't meet that many men on tour, it is surely not for lack of looking, though. We're certainly not as forced about searching out a crowd as the men are, but we keep our eyes open. If there's some cute guy sitting in Section 8 by the far baseline, you can be sure that the word gets quickly back to the locker room to check out the dark-haired guy in the blue sweater just up from the far baseline in Section 8.

I think, as a matter of fact, that we are beginning to feel comfortable in the locker room. A locker room has always sounded like a man's place—even one full of women—and that impression is heightened by the fact that in many of the places where we are assigned to change there are urinals. From everything I hear and read about men's locker rooms, the guys seem to feel so much more at home, talking loudly, snapping towels at each other. Women tend to be much more subdued and private in their locker rooms. In fact, when I got into a regular screaming match with Wendy Turnbull after we played against each other in doubles at Wimbledon in 1979, it occurred to me that that was one of the rare times that anything like that had ever happened. And it was probably very healthy that we got it out of our system, too. I've been better friends with Wendy ever since.

You must keep in mind, though, that in tennis, regardless of gender, a locker room is going to be a different place than one where a team dresses together. After a game in a team sport, everybody in a locker room is in the same boat, victory or defeat, but in a tennis locker room you've got the winner and the loser both there—even side-by-side in some cases. Generally, no matter what is happening with the other players, no matter how much noise or chatter, or no matter how critical we may have been if the match was on television, as soon as those two players come back to the locker room from the match, everybody pretty much clams up, except perhaps for the "Well done" or "Bad luck." And boy, they all took a wide berth with me after I lost.

It is never easy to have to dress with someone you're playing against, but it is part of the sport and something you have to learn to live with. One of the toughest times for me was at Wimbledon in 1973, when Chris and I were playing in the finals. But it rained, and we had to stay there for hours together before the match was finally postponed for a day. Near the end we were just sitting there alone, eating bonbons.

I don't know why, but that night I had an inspiration. I decided to try and play her an entirely different way for the first set. So I stayed back on the baseline, like Chris herself, but unlike her, I threw up all spins and no pace, and it completely discombobulated her and I wiped her out at love. Then in the second set—it was a very windy day, and the lobs would drop out of the sky like badminton shuttlecocks—I went back to my more normal manner, and I just held on to win 7–5. I was absolutely exhausted at the end because all the adrenaline drained out of me—but not from playing. What almost wore me out was the sitting around the locker room with Chris the day before. How do you learn to train for that?

I think it was probably easier in the old days, too, when there weren't so many of us, so we were closer, or, at least, more familiar. It is easier to dress with a friend who just beat you than with a stranger. Also, now that we get more press coverage our "duels" are built up more. In the old days it was easier to forgive and forget because even if something harsh or awkward happened on the court it wasn't liable to involve many more than the two of us playing. We could put it behind us. But now, in a case like the one involving Pam cursing Tracy in Toronto, how will either one ever be allowed to drop it? Every time they're scheduled to play again, the press is going to remind them of Toronto and try to make a grudge fight out of it.

Pam is one of the great locker-room clowns, though. She leads the kind of kidding that is becoming more normal with us. "Hey, who's the flattest around here?" Pam will call out. "Come on, King, you and Wade get over here and line up." And then everybody will give it back to Pam for the silly way she walks like a duck.

Rosie was always like that, too. When Larry promoted the Wightman Cup in Chicago in 1981, he had to check something with the players, so when he knocked on the door, Rosie told him to come on in, that everybody was dressed. But Chris was still in the shower, and as soon as Larry got in the room, Rosie literally dragged him to the showers. Aha, but a couple nights later, Larry came by to see Rosie, who was the team captain, at her hotel room. A couple of the players and Connie Spooner, the trainer, were sitting around, and Connie told Larry that Rosie was in the bathroom and to go on in. The way she said it, he assumed Rosie must be brushing her hair. He opened the door. Rosie was not brushing her hair.

The male players—Aussies particularly—are always asking me who the locker-room "paraders" are. That's what we call the less modest types. I'm not one myself; when I have to move about, I'm almost sure to be prudishly tricked out in my bra and panties. A lot of it is cultural. The Scandinavians never seem to have a stitch on, but the younger girls, like Tracy or Andrea, are always covered up like nuns. I don't think either one of them has ever taken a shower. A lot of the better players are Class A paraders—and you can read whatever you want into that.

Then, when we're ready, dressed for the court, there is one cooperative function we regularly have to perform for each other. "See any red on me?" is the code language. That can be so embarrassing if you're not careful. One time, in the middle of the warm-ups for a doubles match, I started falling apart from laughter when I looked over at my partner. "Hey, I hate to tell you this," I said, "but your string is hanging out." Ooops. And what can you do? Of all the double standards in the world, surely the most unfair one is that men can get away with scratching themselves but women can't. And we get worse itches. There's no justice. That is the one time in my life when I've wanted to be a guy—when I had an itch on the court.

I'm told there used to be an old tennis writer who kept a little book, updating the top players' periods. That was like Clark Graebner, who was always coming up to me in England, where betting is legal, and saying, "Hey, you having your period? Who's on the rag?" But a little knowledge about menstruation can be a dangerous thing. In fact, in my case, the only time my period affected me was two days *before* my period began. Then I would sometimes have a terrible problem with my depth perception.

There is just no pattern of menstruation's effects on female athletes. Some players only get cramps on the first day, some never have any problems whatsoever, and some are only troubled every other month. Poor Rosie probably lost her best shot at the U.S. title in 1968, when she came down with horrible menstrual problems right before she played Virginia in the quarters. Virginia beat Rosie.

In the other half of the draw, I got to the finals, but my knee was absolutely killing me. The night I beat Bueno in the semis in three sets, I had to rest it up over a guitar case I put on the bed, but I still was in such pain I could barely sleep. I was up almost all night crying, and the next day I couldn't move. Virginia jumped all over my serve, and she beat me in straight sets. I'm fairly certain that Rosie would have beaten Virginia if she hadn't had such a bad period, and then I'm sure she would have beaten me for the championship.

There is one thing about the body that I've become more and more convinced of, the older I get: big chests are no good. I am not, however, talking only about females. It seems to me that the single element most overlooked in playing the game is the ability to pivot, and that if you are too thick in the torso you will have more difficulty in managing this. McEnroe has been really heavy in the thighs. But he can twist and turn so well. Everything is involved with the turn.

But ladies, here is a hint: if you are playing a friend who does have big boobs, bring her to the net and make her hit backhand volleys. That's the hardest shot for the well-endowed. "I've got to hit over them or under them, but I can't hit through them," Ann Jones used to moan to me. Not having much of them, I found it hard to sympathize with her.

I will say that I think tennis is a very sexy sport, and that is good. The players are young, with excellent bodies, clothed in relatively little. It offers the healthiest, most appealing presentation of sex I can imagine, and we in the sport must acknowledge that and use it to our advantage. I do not think, for example, that the foundations of the game crumbled any when Linda Siegel came out of her top at Wimbledon in 1979.

Trivia question: Who was playing Linda Siegel then?

First answer: You mean someone else was on the court?

Second answer: Billie Jean King.

I don't mean we should start playing topless. I'm frankly never very comfortable playing in South America, where the old-fashioned Latin machismo attitude prevails. It is not surprising to me that South America keeps turning out excellent male players—Vilas, Clerc, Pecci, Gomez, Gildemeister, etc.—but that that culture has produced only one female player—Bueno—of any consequence. They do not exactly turn out with the proper attitude down there for the women's competition. As soon as you reach for your zipper on your warm-up jacket or begin to take your sweat pants off, the whole crowd starts to whistle. It's hysterical.

The South Americans don't even like it if you show up wearing a knee brace. I'm serious; they don't even like women who are taped. The last time I played in Chile I had a bandage on my thigh, and it was a little cool, anyway, so I played my opening match with my sweat pants on. I knew the Chileans didn't like that. I told the other players that I'd be hearing something. And sure enough, the next morning one of the promoters called me at the hotel. "Mrs. King," he said, "please take off your pants tonight, because we like to look at the ladies' legs."

That is all so ludicrous, it is funny, but I do not agree at all with my friend Janie Blalock, the golf pro, who got all worked up not long ago because one of the other pros, Jan Stephenson, posed for a magazine photo lounging on a bed, with a little bit of leg showing. Somehow, to Janie, this represented a cheapening—a prostitution, if you will—of the game of golf. That's ridiculous. It's just a matter of mutual self-interest. Jan Stephenson happens to be very pretty, as sure as she is a very good golfer, and her displaying that beauty is no more a threat to the integrity of golf than is Jim Palmer's 95-percent-naked body in underwear ads a threat to the good name of baseball.

In the WTA, we try to encourage our players to be as

attractive and as feminine as possible. We urge all our members to wear tennis dresses or skirts, but if somebody like Nancy Gunter or Anne Smith simply can't feel comfortable on the court that way, then shorts are fine. The point is that appearance counts for a lot in any sport, but is perhaps even more important to tennis, where the fans are so close to the players. And certainly we offer something for everyone's physical taste. I remember talking to Dinah Shore not long ago, and she was just raving about Roscoe Tanner's legs. That buffaloed me; I just couldn't see that. Then I remembered that Dinah had that long-term thing with Burt Reynolds, and he's got those same kind of stocky Roscoe-legs.

Myself, I was always more of a Nastase-kind-of-legs girl. Or Roger Taylor. Head to toe. I would have paid money any day to see Roger Taylor play, so I really can't be horribly upset to discover that there are some terrible male chauvinists out there who would buy tickets to see Linda Siegel play.

13 GIRL RACKETS AND BOY RACKETS

One of the great disillusionments in life is finding out what the people at the top are really like. I remember lying in bed one night holding hands with Larry, just talking about all the things that were happening to us in a swirl. This was just about the time I was suddenly being discovered, being decreed fashionable, and doors were opening everywhere. And finally I uttered the unthinkable: how dumb many of these important people were; and we both laughed our bahoolas off.

"Yeah, can you believe it?" Larry said. "Can you believe it?"

"There really is a chance for us," I said.

Of course, I must admit that I came up through such a hypocritical system that it was difficult for me not to be cynical about the people in charge. But then, perhaps it is too polite or innocent for me to suggest that the abuses in tennis, in amateur sports, could be any worse than those in business or politics or television or any other line of work. But I do know this: that when you come from a background of honor and fair labor, as I did, and then are thrust into an environment where "respectable" people of consequence and privilege are cheating and lying as a matter of course, it is a shattering experience—especially for a person so young as a teenager. It is amazing that so many of us tennis players managed to survive the experience as well as we did.

Everything was such a sham. Imagine being a kid, still in your teens, and dickering over the phone with some tournament director for under-the-table appearance money, and then arriving, to be greeted with an envelope full of cash. It felt like something you had seen in the movies, out of a smuggling ring or the rackets. It was such a penny-ante form of soul-selling, though. The most I ever made as an amateur, champion of the world, was $7,000 in 1967, the last year before open tennis finally came in.

Boy, but those USLTA characters could be cheap. I remember once that Larry was placed in the men's draw at the national clay court championships in Milwaukee. This was a U.S. championship, understand, but by slipping Larry in they could save on expenses for one valid male player and justify giving me a little bit more. Of course, it gypped one young man out of getting into a tournament he deserved to play in.

It was this sort of treatment that first got me interested in forming a players' association. In 1965, long before open play came in, it was the policy of the USLTA to pay their own American players $20 a day in expenses at Forest Hills—if you were among the top four Americans seeded. Even in 1965, $20 a day was hardly any king's ransom to survive on in New York, but worse than that, it was common for the USLTA to arbitrarily bump one of their American players out of the seeding spots and move up a foreigner just so they could save a lousy twenty bucks a day. Can you believe it? And of course, at the same time they were paying a foreigner like Maria a huge guarantee under the table to play the Longwood doubles and Forest Hills.

This particular year, Mary Ann Eisel deserved a high seeding on the grass, but they dropped her back further in the pack to save the few dollars, and that really left her distraught, as she certainly should have been. "Come on," I said. "This just isn't fair, no matter how long they've been doing it. We have to protest. We need an association." But neither Mary Ann or anybody else was willing to stick their necks out at that time. If your national association blackballed you, forget it, because you wouldn't be able to play tennis anywhere in the world. The federations all backed each other up.

I'll tell you a funny story in passing. The USLTA would force all American players to come back to the States right after Wimbledon and play in the U.S. events—even if we could get more money and a better growing-up experience playing in Europe. It also would have helped someone like me learn to play on clay earlier. But there was one male U.S. player—just the same lone guy—who was allowed to stay over and play the full European circuit every summer. He went everywhere. And you know what? He was CIA. He was just like the character Robert Culp played, only fifteen years before *I Spy* went on TV.

But short of asking you to be a spook, all the national associations were terribly cynical in appealing to your patriotism. They would create or control some international competition—Davis Cup, Wightman Cup, whatever—and then you, as a player, were automatically expected to stop everything you were doing and, at whatever personal cost, play for "your country." Only, of course, it wasn't really for your country; it was for your federation—the USLTA, the LTA of Britain, the LTAA of Australia, whatever. If you wouldn't play for them, or if you protested at all, then you were nothing short of Benedict Arnold. Not only that, but international competition provided the federation officials with an excuse to fly first-class to some exotic place where they could play a little social tennis themselves, lie in the sun, and generally have a wonderful vacation while we played for our country, allegedly.

I always looked at these matters differently, which is why I was never held dearly by the USLTA. I felt that no matter where I played as an individual, whether at Wimbledon or in the East Cupcake Championships in Jambayla, Mongolia, I was also playing as an American. I do not need a red-white-and-blue uniform and Old Glory flying above the courts to turn me into an official American. I never felt any special pressure when I heard "Advantage, United States" instead of "Advantage, Mrs. King." I always understood that if I lost the set, the White House wasn't going to crumble. I always felt more pressure playing for Billie Jean King as an American than for Billie Jean King as a representative of the USLTA.

It is also true that not everybody in tennis administration was a scoundrel. There were some who even liked me and a few who actually tried to understand me. None, for example, was more sympathetic than Bob Kelleher, who was president of the USLTA in the late sixties and a Davis Cup captain before that (he's now a federal judge in California). Mr. Kelleher was one USLTA official who made some effort to learn about me, and because of that he came to appreciate that I was not just some fire-breathing rebel, that, in fact, there did beat within me the heart of a traditionalist. I don't think he ever fathomed me or comprehended the conflicts within me, but at least he made the effort, and he wanted to help.

At Forest Hills in 1967, he came up to me after I had played an easy early-round match in the Stadium, and he asked if he could go back to the clubhouse with me, and we walked along that little gravel pathway, chatting. I can still hear the gravel crunching under our feet during those long moments of silence between our exchanges. "Billie Jean," Mr. Kelleher said, "I think you can win the Sullivan Trophy this year."

That is the top American honor for an amateur athlete, although most of the time it goes to somebody in an Olympic sport, usually in track and field, and probably someone peaches-and-cream, too. Blacks, for example, almost never win the Sullivan Memorial Trophy; not once between 1961 and 1981. Also, the selectors shied away from tennis, even when it was a major amateur sport. The only tennis player ever to have won the Sullivan had been Don Budge, thirty years before, in 1937. Not Connolly, not Kramer, not Gibson, not Trabert. The USLTA sure would have liked to win a Sullivan again, and since we didn't have any outstanding male players at the time, I was the only game in town.

Mr. Kelleher told me that he was sure they could mount a nice and proper little backstage PR campaign for me, and he was fairly certain I could win. He also told me that he was afraid that there was a move afoot in the USLTA to have me suspended. So, if I would just mind my manners for a few months and keep my mouth shut, I could not only save my skin but probably win the Sullivan Trophy as well. I could tell, too, that Mr. Kelleher really wanted me to win; he was on my side.

But all I could hear then, for the longest time, was that gravel crunching under our feet. I thought about what he had said. I really did. We were approaching the clubhouse by now. Finally, I stopped and turned to him. "I'm sorry, Mr. Kelleher," I said. "I'm sorry, but I can't do it."

Even then it was too late for awards. They always come too late. Randy Matson, the shot-putter, won the Sullivan instead of me.

Mr. Kelleher was the prime mover in making open tennis a reality, too. It began the next year, 1968. But if shamateur tennis is a thing of the past, I know well enough that the same abuses exist wherever amateurism is artificially maintained.

It simply won't work, because in every case what you get is control without risk, and that kind of socialism is bound to doom whatever the enterprise is. The person I'd really like to talk to is William Simon, President Ford's secretary of the treasury, the big kahoona from Wall Street who is always touting free enterprise but who then turns around and, as head of the U.S. Olympic Committee, asks us to support a system where the athletes train for four years in order to be paid off in medals and thrills.

As far as I'm concerned, the very best break we could get would be for the Russians to find some excuse and pay us back for boycotting the 1980 Moscow Games by boycotting the 1984 Los Angeles Olympics. Great; then, right away, we should open up the competition for all athletes, no matter how they earn their money, whether as contract pros or scholarship pros or government pros—whatever.

A lot of people would be horrified and say, Oh, you can't do that, because then the Communist countries would stay out of the competition and you wouldn't have a real world championship. But I'll bet you this: the Soviets and their puppets would bluff for a while, but then they'd jump back in, feet first. Open tennis didn't scare them away, did it? After a lot of fulminating, the Russians were delighted to let players like Olga Morozova and Alex Metreveli compete—just so long as the government could take the lion's share of the purse money.

Tennis in the United States can be made even freer still, too. It's absolutely ridiculous that the best young players are, in effect, frozen out of college, so that they have to choose between developing their game or developing themselves. The time between seventeen and twenty is absolutely crucial to any player, but because so many of the kids at that age are still immature, they would be better off going to college and doing at least some of their playing for the school team—and ideally a Team Tennis squad, where men and women play together. What earthly difference would it make if John McEnroe could play for the Stanford team in the spring and then go off to Wimbledon as an individual?

When Larry and I owned *womenSports* magazine, I urged Mildred Barnes, the head of the Association for Intercollegiate Athletics for Women (AIAW), the women's college sports association, to change the rules for women's sports. Let kids play college and pro at the same time. If you're an actress, you can perform in college theatricals and then work for money in summer stock. If you're a singer, you can join the college glee club and then sing for money in a bar on weekends if you want. What is the difference between a tennis player or a golfer or a baseball player or any other athlete doing the equivalent sort of thing? A college scholarship is simply a contract, and once the college season ends, the player becomes a free agent.

I tried to convince Ms. Barnes that if the AIAW took that step, it would give the AIAW some separate identity and perhaps even force the old fogies in the National Collegiate Athletic Association to change their position. But instead, the AIAW more or less went along with the NCAA, and ultimately, for its reward, pretty much got swallowed up by the NCAA, so now women's athletics will have even less of an independent voice in the United States.

What is so especially ironic about this ridiculous antiprofessionalism, which drives the best players out of college, is that all college sports are suffering through terrible financial times. But if great players like Austin and McEnroe were permitted to play college Team Tennis, the sport could support itself and wouldn't have to go, hat in hand, to the football and basketball people for charity. Women's sports, especially, must be more original in their promotion. I hate to admit it, but the trouble is that women are invariably worst at marketing; we have such a silly bake-sale mentality.

I'll admit that I didn't like the idea of having Virginia

Slims, a cigarette, as our first sponsor for women's pro tennis. I don't like the idea of smoking—smoke physically bothers me—and so it was very hard to accept the deal. But Larry, who is even more adamantly opposed to smoking than I, was the person who convinced me to go along. "Do you believe in the right of a legal product to advertise in a free-enterprise society?" he asked me.

"You know I do."

"Do you think it's right that certain products, like tobacco, are banned from advertising on television?"

"No, I don't think that's right."

"Well, then, Billie Jean, don't you compound that wrong by saying that Virginia Slims can't advertise as a tennis promoter, either."

And Larry was correct. I still don't look with any favor upon cigarettes, but, just as Virginia Slims had promised, neither I nor any other player was ever personally asked to endorse smoking. In fact, one time, when we had a tournament scheduled in a high-school gym in Tennessee, the Slims people made us find a new site because they did not want to display any of their advertising in a place normally associated with teenagers. But what is most important is that Virginia Slims made it possible for women's professional sports to compete, and it provided numerous opportunities for many people that did not exist before. They also, by the way, set a standard for the effective and efficient management of tennis tournaments that raised the entire level of the sport's promotion, the men's as well as the women's.

Every time, give me the pros. Put them in charge and oblige the event to operate on a paying basis, and then I'll accept what happens in the marketplace. Just spare me the amateurs and the do-gooders performing in the name of charity and sacrifice and—look out when you hear this—the good of the game.

I can't stand what the National Football League's players'

union is trying to accomplish now: standardize salaries on the basis of position and time in service. I'm an old union leader—I'm an old union *founder*—but I say players' unions should be in business to make sports more free and open, not locked into some anti-incentive socialistic system such as that. Shortly after I heard about that union plan, when I was in Washington, I met Ed Garvey, who is the head of the NFL players' association, the man behind the idea, and I really blew my stack at him. "You're a socialist. What you're planning just won't work!" I screamed.

Poor Garvey, he didn't know what hit him.

People sneer that tennis is "subsidized," that its economic viability is somehow suspect because corporations such as Avon and Toyota and Volvo and Playtex underwrite many tournament guarantees. But it's nonsense to argue like that. Are these companies investing money in a sport out of the goodness of their hearts? Of course not. They've obviously made a hardheaded business decision that tennis is one good way to spend their money and promote their product. You might as well say that television is subsidized, or the World Series is, because Miller Beer or Right Guard buys commercial time to sponsor a game.

In the same way, I'm irritated by the holier-than-thou types who think it soils tennis if popular players are guaranteed appearance money. The argument is that if you pay someone like Borg up-front money to play in your tournament, then he is not likely to knock himself out on the court to try and win more of the prize money. Human nature being what it is, I suppose that could always be the case with some players. It is also true that a superstar like Steve Garvey hustled his bahoola off in the play-offs and World Series in 1981 just to make a lousy few thousand more bucks, which, in his tax bracket, wouldn't even make a dent.

My point is, if I'm a tournament director and I have an advertising budget of, say, $50,000, and I choose to spend

$25,000 of that to get Borg to play and most of the other $25,000 to publicize that he is playing, then how does this hurt any other player?

Obviously, my own ox is being gored here. I'm at that stage of my career where I'm more valuable as a drawing card than as a competitor. In any tournament I play in, the chances are that I would be defeated in one of the early rounds, yet I would stir up more interest in the tournament and sell a substantial number of tickets—well over any amount I might take out of the tournament in prize money. By the same token, there are a lot of young players who are better than I, who make $100,000 or more a year, but who have no name value at the box office. Let me come in on a guarantee, and the extra fans that I draw might well go away remembering some of these newer players.

Economically, guarantees are where the market is right now. It goes back to free enterprise. It also amuses me when people suggest that someone like Bjorn can be guaranteed to appear at a shopping center or at a resort or at a hotel because he is a famous tennis player, but he cannot be paid guarantees to appear on a tennis court. Now what kind of sense does that make? Player guarantees are just another reflection of a free marketplace, that's all.

And always, of course, as I tell the young players, sports is about the toughest career a woman can choose. Marriage, for example: how many men are prepared to sacrifice their own career in order to travel with you? Children? The normal career woman can afford to give up a couple years here or there to take time out, a sabbatical, to have children. But for an athlete the prime years of competition conflict directly with the childbearing years. If you take off from tennis to have a family, you may be giving up 20 percent of your playing career. And because women are newer to sports than to other endeavors, they are more often alone, without the usual support. I've pointed out to the young players coming into the sport that there are virtually no women executives in tennis—just Ella Masolino, Edy McGoldrick, Nancy Jeffett, maybe one or two others. The only one who ever really made it to the very top was Gladys Heldman, and it is instructive that she didn't do it within the structure. Nobody promoted her. She went outside the Old Boy system and did it on her own, creating the magazine *World Tennis*.

I learned the hard way in the racket racket. I always was very loyal to Wilson, from the time they gave me my first racket, and in fact, I was the first champion ever to play with their aluminum model, the T-2000, when they first brought it out. I won Wimbledon with it in 1967, years before Connors appeared on the scene, and then, that September, I won the U.S. nationals, and Clark Graebner, the first important man to use it, got to the finals against Newcombe. We made an absolute sensation of that racket. But Wilson wouldn't pay me anything extra for my risk, for being their guinea pig, and when open tennis came in, all they agreed to do for me was to kick up my fee from $500 to $1,500.

I was the top player in the world then, but Wilson refused to sell an autographed model with my name on it, because they were already making a Maureen Connolly "woman's racket." The Connolly model was exactly the same as the Wilson best-seller, the Jack Kramer model, but Wilson carried on as if there were all the difference in the world between a man's racket and a woman's. The way they talked sometimes, you would think the woman's racket could have babies. But finally I went to Gene Buick, the Wilson racket manager, and I flat-out asked him why they couldn't produce a Billie Jean model. Maureen was very sick then. "If Maureen dies, sure," he said. "Only one woman at a time." I couldn't believe he had said that; I almost got sick.

Not long after that, Maureen did die, and Wilson began producing a Billie Jean model. And then, not long after that, the tennis boom hit, which should have been a bonanza for me, but instead, the Old Boy crowd squeezed me out. The supply couldn't keep up with the demand, so they set almost all the molds for the two men's rackets, the Kramer and the Stan Smith, and production of the Billie Jean fell relatively off, even as more people were buying rackets.

I complained to Wilson about how they shortchanged me, but it never did any good. The whole system was stacked. One day, I came in to visit a sporting-goods store in Dayton, Ohio, just as a young boy was asking the salesman for a Billie Jean King model, and I heard the salesman (who hadn't noticed me) tell the kid that he shouldn't get a girl's racket. So he sold him a Stan Smith model, when, in fact, the only difference in the rackets were the name decals.

Another problem I had with being a female pioneer is that that made some women think they owned me. Gee, sometimes I didn't know what was worse, being cheated and ignored by the men or smothered and used by the women. So many of the more outspoken feminists really had so little in common with me. They were liberal Democrats who couldn't stand to see anybody make a profit. And long-winded? Unfortunately, I found out that every stale old joke about women talking too much was proved out by the women's movement. Show me a short memo, I'll show you a man who wrote it.

Often I disliked the feminists because they were so doctrinaire. I was supposed to agree to their whole agenda, but I simply don't fall into any neat niche. For example, while I'm completely, 100 percent in favor of the right to choose an abortion and opposed to the no-choice people, I am generally a conservative. In fact, the only reason I support the Equal Rights Amendment is for the strict conservative reason that at the time the Constitution was drawn up, women had no rights of franchise or property, and I think it is important to technically rectify that.

Above all, I believe that this country is built upon freedom of choice. And that has made it hard for me. Especially at the

time when I was a cult figure, and everybody lumped me—
the Feminist Athlete Doll—with Jane Fonda and Gloria
Steinem and Betty Friedan and Bella Abzug, I really was
personally shying away from some women's groups because I
believed that they were trampling upon choices even as they
protested that women were being trampled upon.

I remember one horrible occasion when some especially
strident feminists called me up at my hotel and demanded
ten press tickets for the tournament I was playing in. Ten!
And they didn't qualify as press in any way whatsoever. I
explained that as politely as I could, and then finally agreed
that I would go against my best judgment and arrange to
have one press credential left. And then, at the matches,
two women showed up and started making a fuss about how
they were being discriminated against when they were only
offered the one seat. That sort of thing drove me crazy
regularly.

As always, you see, I was the maverick, not willing to
accept completely the dictates of any particular group. The
feminists couldn't understand why I wouldn't go along completely with them, on their terms; but in tennis, there I was
presumed to be a crazy revolutionary. Isn't it funny that you
can be alone in the middle?

I remember one early meeting of the WTA, in Detroit, and I
was talking, and I guess I was rambling on, because the
Australian player Lesley Hunt stood up and interrupted me
and, very nicely, told me to shut up. In fact, it was about the
best put-down I ever got, because Lesley was correct and
firm, but she was very affectionate, too. What she said was
"Okay, Billie Jean, that's enough. You've got to remember
that when you were a little girl you used to sit on a rock and
dream all these dreams. But that was just you. Please understand. Please don't get angry at us that we didn't sit on that
rock with you. We didn't have your dreams."

I4 PLAYING FOR THE LOVE OF IT

I'm sure that one reason why Wimbledon always meant so much to me was because I associated the United States championships with the USLTA. The British Lawn Tennis Association might not have been any better to play for, but I didn't have to play for it. And then, Wimbledon was the first place I ever played out of the country, and it was everything I imagined; and not only that, but it became a dream for me, because Karen and I won the doubles that first year I was there, 1961. It was heaven.

Karen and I stayed up past two that night, shoving many of the things we had into little carry-on bags so that we could make the weight allowance with our regular luggage, and then we got to the airport and everybody recognized us and just waved us through. It didn't matter how much luggage we had. We were champions, celebrities. Oh, that was heady.

The British loved me then. I was young and chubby, Little Miss Moffitt and all that. And I was an entertaining r/u. My

162

second year there, I upset Margaret in the first round, when she was seeded number one, but then I got beat myself; I knew my place. The romance began to unravel in 1966, when I became a winner. The month before, on Centre Court, I had also triumphed in the key match in the Wightman Cup. I beat Annie Jones 5–7, 6–2, 6–3. I shouldn't even have played that day. I had virtually no circulation in one knee, and when I finally got going and turned the match around, the British screamed—I mean they literally yelled it out—that I had been playing possum, faking a cramp. And then I won my first Wimbledon singles right after that, and the next year I beat Annie in the finals, and by then they were turning against me. The British really disliked me then until I started getting old and couldn't play very well anymore, and then they decided that I was an r/u again, so it was all right to like me once more. That's the way it goes.

But I'll be perfectly honest: the British hurt me a great deal in 1981. I was there, working for NBC, but it was the first time I hadn't played at Wimbledon in twenty years. They made a big fuss over Virginia's twentieth Wimbledon, which was fine, because she's a native; and also, in the years before that, they had celebrated Maria and Margaret when they returned after retiring. But for me, the one with the record twenty titles—nothing. I tell you, I would have loved it if somebody had invited me to sit in the Royal Box for one day. Just once. Just one gesture like that. It would have meant a lot to me. Oh, well . . .

I guess the British never understood me, never fathomed my sense of tradition—a belief in an ongoing, living tradition, not a dead one. I remember after I won in 1973, and I was being interviewed behind some little table that was covered with a Union Jack, and one of the photographers called out for me to pose with my feet up on the table, and I started to go along, and then I said, "No, that would be disrespectful to the flag."

And the clubman who was my escort, a classic old Wimbledon type, just about keeled over. "Why, Mrs. King, that's so very thoughtful of you," he said.

Two years later, Arthur and I won, and that was a very special night for me. I made something of a fuss by telling Wimbledon that unless two very important people I knew were invited to the victory ball, then I wouldn't come.

The two people were Mr. and Mrs. Twyman. He was the chief groundskeeper for many years there, and Mrs. Twyman was the main attendant in the ladies' locker room. But, of course, they weren't members of the club, so nobody had ever thought to invite them before. They were just thrilled, and when I mentioned them in my speech, I looked out into the crowd and saw that they both had tears in their eyes.

No, I don't think the British have any notion of how much I love that wonderful tennis place of theirs. Why, there isn't a year I've come back when I haven't gone out to Centre Court a day or two before the tournament begins, to just stand there by myself, staring down at the grass, communing with the surroundings, and thinking of all the people who've played there. I don't mean only the champions. I imagine all the first-round losers who were lucky enough to get the chance to stride onto Centre Court.

In 1977, when Virginia reached the finals against Betty Stove, it became apparent in the third set that she was finally going to win Wimbledon—Our Ginny, champion of the Wimbledon Centenary. Mrs. Twyman had retired, and another lovely British lady, Mrs. Fraser, had taken her place in the locker room. I was watching the match on television with her, and suddenly I grabbed her by the hand. "Come on," I said, "you've got to see your girl win this in person." I led Mrs. Fraser up to the players' section, and as Virginia was serving out the last points, I actually said—I remember this, verbatim: "Mrs. Fraser, this script was written in heaven." And then she started crying, and by the end I had tears of happiness in my eyes for the British and for Our Ginny and for their Wimbledon.

Virginia and I were never all that close, either. Also, the older she got, the more gamesmanship she developed. One time, warming up with Martina before their match, Virginia didn't give her a single ball to her backhand. Martina won, but she was still fuming long after the match. Another time, in Boston a few years ago, Rosie got so mad at Virginia that when they shook hands at the net, Rosie started screaming at her, and then—get this—she wouldn't let go of Virginia's hand. It was like the Tar Baby. Virginia would keep trying to pull her hand away, and Rosie wouldn't let her let go.

The trouble was, as Virginia got older and began to lose some of her talent, she started stalling a lot: wanting to discuss everything with the umpire, pacing about, hitting balls into the net after a point—all that sort of thing. I've always been able to accept that type of behavior when I knew it wasn't a put-on. Tory Fretz used to walk around in circles, and she'd never catch a ball, even if it was hit right to her. Kathy Jordan is a hothead, like me, who can blow off steam at any time. But in cases like that, the behavior is part of the normal procedure. What bugged me about the stuff Virginia started to pull was that it was contrived.

Of course, she was always too twitchy and nervous—high-strung the wrong way, just as McEnroe is high-strung right. But never say that Virginia Wade didn't have guts and didn't try. She had those great, wide shoulders, too. In fact, when we were on the New York Apples together, our dresses were absolutely identical in size except that they had to sew in two extra panels for her shoulders. She went absolutely as far as she could with what she was given, except she never really did gain a good court sense. Virginia had a fine first serve and forehand, but she couldn't hit anything down the line. I fed her junk all the time. But it didn't matter what the score; she'd never pack it in, never stop going for it.

Rosie was a lot like Virginia in that one way—that she was always dead honest on the court. And, of course, she was so entertaining. It did sort of irritate me when people wrote all that junk about Rosie getting psyched out by me when it counted. What was all the mumbo-jumbo? I was not only a much better player than Rosie, but she was also much lazier.

I often told her—and remember, we were doubles partners for seven straight years—that if she was going to try and play the net game, as short as she was, even far shorter than I, then she was going to have to be five times better conditioned than anybody else. But she didn't want to hear that. Rosie was quite content being number five or six in the world. For as much as she always knocked herself out on the court, she just wouldn't do what was necessary in preparation. She'd rather have a good time with all her friends. You know what Rosie loves the best in all the world? Amusement parks. I'll bet she's been to every one on the face of the earth that's worth anything.

For that matter, Rosie and I have played just about everywhere in the world, too, because the two of us—and Annie Jones and Frankie Durr—made up the female complement of the long-forgotten National Tennis League. Rosie was only twenty when she signed, and she took a lot of heat for that, because it was considered bad enough for a woman to become a professional, but even worse, she hadn't put in years of poverty before selling her soul.

I signed for $40,000, which sounds like it was a lot at that time—and it was. Unfortunately, I never made the $40,000, because there was also a system of percentage versus guarantee, and the percentages were guaranteed more than the guarantees, and even if I won every match, the winning percentage couldn't add up to $40,000. The head of the NTL was George MacCall, whose other claim to fame was that he had been the Davis Cup captain when the United States got beaten by Ecuador. That was one "George story." Soon we all had collections of George stories. "You know George," we would say. But George was a nice guy, and I was so happy to be a pro.

My first professional match on the tour was in Cannes. The Riviera! What an omen, what a place to start! Yeah, and you know where on the Riviera we played? In a high-school gym. It was pouring rain outside and so stuffy in there that my glasses got all steamed up and I could barely see. Vic Braden was there, working for the NTL, and Vic had traveled all over the world for years on the various Kramer tours. "Welcome to the pros!" he screamed at me.

"Take me back to the country clubs!" I hollered back. But I loved it. At last I was a pro. Play-for-pay.

George always talked big. He flew first-class and smoked a huge stogie, and he was forever promising us that he was some night going to spring for a huge dinner for his girls. And sure enough, one night at last, we were in London with no matches scheduled, and George phoned from Paris and said he was flying right over and for Rosie and me to get dressed up and meet him at the Guinea, which is a really nice restaurant in the West End. So we got all dolled up—I can still see Rosie in her best pink dress—and we took a cab to the Guinea, asked for Mr. MacCall's table, and waited. And waited. Since neither Rosie or I are drinkers, what could we do—knock back Shirley Temples all night? Finally, a call from George. He is, unavoidably, still in Paris, but just this moment about to step foot on the plane. Go ahead and order.

We did. We ate. We ordered dessert. We ate that. We waited. No George. Finally, we reached into our purses, nervously, and came up, between us, with just enough to cover the tab, without hardly a farthing left over for the tip. And we had to walk home. I think it was a couple days later when George finally got to London and started talking about how he had to take his girls out to dinner one night. George never changes.

But there was a wonderful camaraderie in the NTL. The men, mostly Aussies—Laver, Stolle, Emerson, Rosewall—plus Gonzales and Andres Gimeno, treated us four women magnificently. In fact, they not only treated us all like one of the guys, they treated us even better, because no matter how much we protested, they would never let us pick up a check. They included us in everything, and not only made us feel so much a part of the tour, but a part of tennis tradition. Besides, we were joined in adversity. A typical NTL day would end around two o'clock in the morning, with a six-o'clock wake-up call so we could be at the airport at seven to get on the eight-o'clock flight. Then somehow, for some reason, wherever we disembarked from the plane, we had a six-hour drive ahead of us. You know George.

We played some dandy spots, too. One night we worked some little town in the Po valley. It was an outdoor match, but a ceiling—with lights—had been constructed directly over the court—although not very high over it. The bad news was that the court was asphalt, freshly laid. Not only that, but whoever had been hired to put down a tennis court had done exactly that: there was a drop-off of about four inches all around the court, from the baselines to the sides past the doubles lines. When you served, you had to hop up onto the court. Well, one thing: it did cut down on foot faults.

Annie Jones—Annie Oakley—and I played. (Rosie had tagged her "Annie Oakley" after she went riding at Maureen Connolly's place in Texas one time, and fell off.) Ann and I should have done what the men on the old-time tours did a lot in the doubles when they got way out in the sticks. They would play two out of three sets, as advertised, only with the private understanding that it was really best of one. Whoever lost the first set, playing all out, also had to tank the second. But Ann and I got all cranked up, and she was chipping and slicing, serving and hopping, with a vengeance. The balls grew as big as pineapples and as black as olives after they hit that asphalt a few times, but we kept at it and ended up going three long sets.

I've told the kids today about these adventures, and I've also told them that I think they would have had to adjust to endure what we did. But then, a lot of my generation played it cozy, too. Nobody was ever more careful than Margaret Smith Court. She wouldn't step over and be a pro with Virginia Slims until we were firmly established as the only major women's tour. Then Margaret popped in and pocketed more than $200,000, which wouldn't have been so bad except that any time anybody would ask her about it, she would say that the money didn't mean a thing to her and that "I only play for the love of it." The first time I heard her say that in an interview, I just about swooned. Pass-out time! No one was worse than Margaret about money. The whole Bobby Riggs thing got started only because Margaret found herself offered $10,000 to play him for the love of it. And, of course, she snapped at it and he destroyed her and then I had to play him myself.

But God, what a champion she was! What an athlete! Margaret was so good that she was naturally a left-hander who simply picked up playing right-handed because it was convenient. She was so fast that I often heard about a pickup race she had against Betty Cuthbert, who had been the Olympic gold medalist in 1956 in both the 100 and 200 meters. At the start, Cuthbert, who knew the ropes of racing, jumped way out in front, but by the finish she was barely a step in front, and they say Margaret would have overtaken her in just a few more paces. Margaret stood about five foot eleven, but she was so long limbed that in terms of reach she was, essentially, six-two. Rosie named her "The Arm."

She also was incredibly strong—if not so strong as Martina today. It was curious. In most respects Margaret was so old-fashioned, just a big old pleasant, thrifty, easygoing, religious farm girl, but in her training she was incredibly sophisticated, far ahead of her time. She was the first female athlete I ever *heard* of who lifted weights, and, looking back to the sixties, she was the only one of us who had any real sense of physical fitness.

In a way, though, she was such a physical specimen that

she didn't have to extend herself on the courts. Margaret never did bother to learn to come over her backhand, just being content to slice it, but she really drove through her forehand; she was so strong she could hit a harder forehand just slapping the ball than any other woman could slugging it, and she had as good a first serve as I ever faced. Yet there was that odd incompleteness to Margaret. She was a front-runner. And, in a very curious way, she was responsible for creating the monster—me—that cost her complete domination of her era.

There was a wealthy businessman in Australia named Bob Mitchell, a great tennis fan, and he heard about this diamond-in-the-rough, and he brought Margaret in out of the boondocks. Mitch told me that when she first came to stay with him, she literally didn't know how to eat or to speak properly. He was her social Pygmalion, and he got Frank Sedgman to polish her on the court. But Mitch soured on Margaret because he didn't think she was appreciative enough of all that he had done for her. That was the prime reason why he invited me to come down to Australia and study with Mervyn Rose. He wanted me to learn to beat the champion he had helped make.

From the start, though, even before Mitch took an interest in me, there was a certain sort of mysticism surrounding Margaret and me. Nothing so strange as this ever happened to me before or since, but in the winter of 1961 I suddenly had a flash that I would play Margaret in the first round of Wimbledon the next June. I came home and told my parents, and they just laughed and said that was fine, but I better stop worrying about Wimbledon and concentrate more on things at hand.

I was attending L.A. State then. I worked out with the boys' tennis team that spring, even did some football agility drills. It was all very casual, no tournaments to speak of. I just sort of popped over to England a few days before Wimbledon. I was practicing on Court 3 at The Queen's Club a couple days after I got there, when all of a sudden I heard a voice coming from the clubhouse. "Billie Jean, Billie Jean!" I stopped and looked. It was Gerry Williams, the British writer.

"What is it?" I called back.

"They just had the draw," Gerry said, "and you'll never guess, but—"

"Sure," I said, very coolly, "I know. I play Margaret in the first round."

And Gerry's face just collapsed. "But they just had the draw. How in the world could you know?"

At that time, too, I had no business on the same court with Margaret. She was a much better player than I until Rose redid my game two years later. But Carole Caldwell and I talked it over and plotted for me to play Margaret's forehand, and I got hot at 2–5 in the third. I held my serve for 3–5, but she went up 30–15, two points from the match, and then I ripped a backhand down the line past her forehand. That was one of those moments that change everything. Margaret was so rattled by that shot that she was dead in the water for the rest of the match and couldn't win another game, and if afterward Margaret often did beat me, it was a different way of life from then on. She knew something else now, and it wouldn't ever be the same against me.

I always loved playing Margaret. In the later years, I had the same sort of feelings whenever I played Chris, because usually, when we did meet, it was for all the marbles. But if I had to choose my favorite opponent, it wouldn't be either Margaret or Chris. It would be Evonne Goolagong Cawley.

I always played my best against Evonne because she always raised her game against me and because she used such spin and variety that it forced me to be more imaginative. It's true that Evonne would sometimes lack concentration and try crazy shots, but I always thought that that part of her was exaggerated by the press because they liked Evonne so much and sought to make excuses for her.

I mean, Evonne was perfect for the press. She was pretty

and exciting to watch and unpredictable, and she won enough without winning all the time. Curiously, though, she was never as popular with the fans as she was with journalists. In this respect, Evonne always sort of brought Arthur Ashe to my mind. Like her, he was an exciting player, but a placid soul; but he was always a better draw than Evonne was, probably because he was American and was so well defined a personality. The fans never seemed to get a handle on what Evonne was really like, so she only made a good gate attraction as an opponent. And she always put up a good match—against me, anyway. She could be very competitive when she put her mind to it, and I think she enjoyed our matches as much as I did.

That time I beat Evonne love and one in the Wimbledon finals (of '75) she really played quite well. She never once lost her concentration that I could tell. But of course, afterward the press all wrote the same junk about her having one of her walkabouts. The fact is that Evonne had three very real chances to sneak back into the match, and in each case she was psychologically all there, but I just blew her away each time with my pace.

In 1971 she beat me in the semis at Wimbledon—three and four; she just passed me at will, it seemed—and then went on to take the title when she was only nineteen. So that was a very special moment for her. And two of the very best matches I ever played were against Evonne. In 1973, in another semifinal at Wimbledon, I needed eight match points before I finally beat her. We both simply played magnificently that day. Nothing daunted us.

On any grass surface, too, you are always vulnerable to a bad break, a lousy bounce (or none at all). In fact, when tiebreakers came in, I adapted to that procedure so easily, I think, because I decided to approach a tiebreaker pretty much the way I play on grass, which is to gamble usually only when you have a two-point cushion. In a tiebreaker, as on grass, I played to expect the unexpected; then, when the unexpected happened, I wasn't rattled. But often ignored in all the whining about Wimbledon's imperfect surface is the fact that its background is the best. There is some solace in being able to see bad bounces; what good does it do you if you can't pick out a ball bouncing perfectly, as is the case on a lot of courts? At Wimbledon, in their somber mauve and green shades, even the ball boys and ball girls blend into the background so perfectly. With my eyes, that was another, more practical reason I loved the place so.

And you know the real difficulty with the noise at the U.S. Open now? It isn't the noise per se, and no matter how high the decibel count of some airliner passing right overhead. That noise builds naturally; you can see it coming, in effect. No, the problem is that having played in a quiet atmosphere all our lives, we tennis players have come to depend on *hearing* our opponent hit the ball. And suddenly when we can't, either from an ear-shattering airplane or a crowd that simply buzzes too loud, we are deprived of a very important sense—and even if we never realized we were using it before. The player who doesn't hear her opponent hit the ball at a place like Flushing Meadow is almost surely going to misjudge the opponent's shots unless she can force herself to use her eyes better, to tell from sight rather than sound how fast and with what spin a ball is coming toward her. Baseball players are set in one place for the pitch, of course, so they can focus better, but they are far more advanced than tennis players at "picking up" pitches. Since there is no sound of a thrown ball, batters have always had to depend strictly on their vision.

Anyway, the other terrific match I played against Evonne was at Forest Hills in 1974, the year after our great Wimbledon three-setter. In this one, I beat her 7–5 in the final set, and after I was down the first set, too. Maybe I am proudest of all of this one, because I almost didn't even enter the tournament that year. I had devoted myself so completely to World Team Tennis, and I was absolutely exhausted. Olga Morozova beat me at Wimbledon earlier in the summer.

But at the last minute I just said, To heck with it, let's give Forest Hills a shot, and my guardian angels got me through. I can hardly recall a single shot in the final against Evonne. I was that tired. I know I adjusted in some way after she took the first set from me at three, but I haven't got a clue to what it was that I did.

Now everyone is saying that Hana Mandlikova is especially reminiscent of Evonne. She will try foolish things on the court, as Evonne did, but it is also true that Hana possesses a much more consistent desire. Evonne liked the idea of being number one every now and then, but she certainly didn't have a fetish about it. It was just a sometime thing, like going on a diet or something. But Hana wants desperately to be champion, and will make the effort to that end, I'm sure. I think, too, with Betty Stove as her coach she has a great advantage. Betty knows where the sport has been, and she has taught Hana what makes up the whole game.

Betty was a mercurial player, not unlike Hana, except with nowhere near as much talent, but she is a very stolid, private person who can sound almost too harsh and judgmental at times. Above all, though, Betty is a sweet person. You know she cares—a good person to have as a coach when you're as young as Hana. I'll never forget that when I had one of my knee operations Betty was one of a handful of players thoughtful enough to remember; she sent me a note and a book about windmills. For most of us on such a global merry-go-round, it is out of sight, out of mind. It is not that we are cold and heartless, but more the other way around; that to be young and a woman and a great athlete today is so exhilarating that it is hard to think of real lives full of normal, everyday things—much less things like hospitals.

I remember a few years ago, when Betty and I were playing

doubles in Japan, and I heard her tell the press early on that she was buying herself a new flat in the Netherlands and that she hoped to do well in this tournament so she could use the prize money to redo the kitchen. That was so basic a vision that it brought all our matches in focus as never before. If I hit a winner, I'd cry out, "There, Betty, there's a skillet." Or, "A new pot." Or after we won a set, I'd tell her, "There, your new stove." Gee it was fun. And Betty got her kitchen.

15 CRYING IN THE SHOWER

Now, if all of us hadn't become lady tennis players, then what? Margaret would have been a preacher, I think. Rosie would have run a traveling carnival, Betty would have been a CPA, Hana a sprinter, and Evonne a housewife who painted on the side instead of a housewife who played tennis on the side. Tracy, Pam, and Andrea would have been teenagers, and Martina would have been the American Dream—whatever that may be. And I? I would have been, naturally, a dancer, with long, willowy legs. Or a rock star. Finally, Chris. She would have been a high-fashion model, I'm sure, and she wouldn't have married a tennis player named John Lloyd because she never would have met him at *Vogue*, but she would have married someone every bit as handsome as John, and just as sweet, and, in either case, Chris would live—will live—happily ever after.

Very few people, I think, understand how fervently this woman wants what she wants. She is a much more determined person than the ruffles and the ribbons that people see on the court. I do think that lately Chris has grown more honest about her intentions, admitting how much she really does care about winning and her place in history. Still, her whole experience is one of playing it safe and, more often than not, doing what she thinks she should do instead of what she wants to do. That is not said unkindly. We happen to be different in this one way, for I grew up with something that my father often said ringing in my ear: "Shouldisms aren't worth shit." And I became an Ayn Rand freak, especially *Atlas Shrugged* and *The Fountainhead*. I came to believe—cynically, you may say—that people are going to try and hurt me precisely through the things I love the most. They are going, specifically, to try and reach me through tennis. Okay, so I figure I might as well lay things on the line just as I believe.

It was Larry who first really began to understand Chris; that she was brought up in such a neat and protected environment, that she would be unlikely to risk herself in the pursuit of some common goal—especially if it might be controversial, much less unpopular. Yet there is so much that Chris and I do share, and there is so much in her that I like and admire. She was always bright and charming; she could talk well in private even when she was a teenager, although it took some time and maturity for that to show itself in public.

When she first descended on the scene, at Forest Hills in 1971, when she was sixteen, beating another one of us grown-ups every day, the other players grew quickly jealous of Chris—even scared of her, I would say. "Look," I told the others, "she's great for us, great for the game." Here, all our lives we had fought for women's tennis, and all of a sudden—hallelujah!—everybody was more interested in women's tennis than in the men's (we were bumping the men in the newspapers day after day), but the players were hurt and upset because a newcomer had popped in out of the blue and was getting all *our* publicity. It just didn't seem fair.

I talked to Chris and tried to be friendly, and I told her

about how I, too, had exploded into the public consciousness once upon a time—Little Miss Moffitt—even though it hadn't been anything approaching this magnitude. But at least I understood better than anybody else what she was starting to go through. We were strolling along that same crunchy gravel path where Mr. Kelleher and I had walked and talked four years before, and I said, "Look, Chris, enjoy this, enjoy every moment of it, because you're on the crest of a wave and there's never going to be anything like this for you again for as long as you live—no matter what else you do and how good you become. Love this!"

And for a high-school kid from a sheltered existence, I think she understood me pretty well. She's always told me that she never forgot that little speech of mine to her.

But then the worm turned. By the time I had to face Chris in the semifinals, a monster had been created, and I had to put an end to it. Now, understand: nothing personal. Just political, just ideological. At that moment in 1971 it was critical that someone defeat Chris because, I'm sure, if she had won Forest Hills her victory would have pretty much destroyed the Virginia Slims tour and women's professional tennis. It would have handed control of the women back to the USLTA—which had already proved that it wanted to keep women in the Dark Ages.

Virginia Slims was not yet a year old, and though our tour was building, it was far from the major success it would become. The USLTA had created its own tour to throw against Slims, and while there was no question but that Philip Morris could outpromote the USLTA, the fact is that the other tour had, frankly, a better collection of players. Margaret, Virginia, and Evonne (who had won Wimbledon that summer) all had thrown in their lot with the USLTA. We were lucky that none of them were Americans, and I was the best draw in women's tennis, but if Chrissie beat me and all the other bad rebels and then joined the USLTA tour (which was her stated intention), the Slims was left with a bunch of r/u's. Well-promoted r/u's, but r/u's all the same.

So you can see that this match against Chris meant far more to me than any other, including the Riggs extravaganza. If I had lost to Chrissie at Forest Hills, so much more would have been affected. If she had beaten me, and then beaten Rosie in the finals, I think that the whole face and future of women's tennis would have been substantially altered.

Obviously, this was a tremendous amount of baggage for me to lug onto the court, while Chris had nothing to burden her. The crowd, of course, was all for her. The pressure: none. She had absolutely nothing to lose. Psychologically, too, she was on a tear, having won forty-six straight matches, and especially after she had survived those six match points against Mary Ann Eisel, there was an air of invincibility about her that she couldn't help but sense. Not only that, but even though she was the challenger, the unknown, we had played once before, in Florida in the spring, and not only had she won, but I had quit. (In fact, I was dehydrated that day because it was right after I had my abortion, and I shouldn't have been playing, but Chrissie didn't know any of that.) In sum, she walked on the court at Forest Hills without any pressure, but secure in the knowledge that she could win. Is there any better frame of mind in which to enter a match?

Before I play, I always take a nice long shower and wash my hair—except at Wimbledon, where they have private baths instead. This day, before I went out to the Stadium to play Chris, I can remember so well standing there in the shower, the hot water running over me, but shaking and crying with fright, out of control. Certainly, I've cried after some tough losses. And, for that matter, I know Chris has, too—but the same as I, alone, briefly. But this time was the only one, ever, when I cried before a match. For comparison, before I played Riggs I actually went to a party an hour or so before the match. I just needed to relax then, which is usually the case. For Chris, I needed strength.

I can still see myself standing there in the shower, bawling, shaking, watching the water swirl down the drain, and thinking, Yeah, just like that, there goes women's tennis and everything else I ever wanted. The symbolism was too obvious to avoid.

Well, as we all know, I survived. I met the threat and turned it back. I got on top and pressed Chris and whipped her in straight sets, and beat Rosie in straights the next day, too, so the Slims had the U.S. champion after all.

Shortly after Forest Hills was finished, too, when Chris was back in school and things had calmed down some, Larry and I flew down to Fort Lauderdale at our own expense and tried to convince Jimmy Evert, Chris's father, to reconsider and let her play on the Slims tour. But we never got to first base with him. He wasn't going to expose her, especially against the establishment, and Chris pretty much went along with that line of thought once she started making her own decisions.

This irritated me at the time, but now I have more of a frame of reference because so many young players have come on tour since then, and I see how natural it is for them to be so influenced by their parents or coaches. Chris herself was very lucky because all the players liked her mother, Colette, who traveled with her; if anything, in fact, Mrs. Evert was accepted as a friend on the tour before Miss Evert was.

Acceptance for Tracy has come much slower. Part of that is simply the matter of age. Chris became a contender at sixteen; Tracy was already a champion by then. Also, some of the players have been slow to take to Mrs. Austin—Jeanne. Myself, I think she's terrific—and what a change in Tracy's childhood from her own. Jeanne told me once that her parents wouldn't even let her climb trees, much less be a professional athlete. And finally, as you can imagine, it is more difficult for any winner to be liked—especially one who achieved so much success so very early. I notice that the other players are so quick to condemn Tracy for superficial things that they tolerate in lesser players.

Tracy has also had, for a champion, a curious problem of public identity. As a player, she's viewed as just another Evert clone. As a person, she suffers some by comparison with Andrea Jaeger, who is younger but more easygoing and gregarious. Tracy is not easy to communicate with. I used to call her "Why" because that is all she ever seemed to say. But on the court I think she is extraordinary. What I like about her is that she plays; she is much more the professional than players who are considerably older. She is also one young player with a great sense of tennis history. In elementary school she did a term paper about Laver and me, called my mother up and everything, and was really angry when she only got an A–. In time, like Chris, I'm sure Tracy will get her due.

Now, with Chris, regardless of her tennis politics, I always felt a bond—did from the moment I walked into her house in Fort Lauderdale. It was eerie, exactly as if I was walking into my own parents' house a continent away. Rosie, a dispassionate observer, who has been in both houses—Bill and Betty's, and Jimmy and Colette's—even says that everything seemed to be in the same places. And I know one thing for sure: in both houses you could feel the discipline in the air.

I'm sure that the reason why Chris was so close to me when she first started to tour was because she sensed how much of a common background we shared. And we both happen to be total competitors and perfectionists. We are eleven years and a month apart in age, and for young athletes a decade is a millennium, so it is quite rare for two rivals to become friends in the face of such an age disparity. But then, always with Chris, I've sensed that one second we were close but in another she'd be far away again. She's like that.

Obviously, some of that has to do with the fact that we were so competitive. Years ago, Nancy Richey Gunter stopped having any sort of personal contact with me so that, she thought, she could deal with me more directly and coldly on the court. And Kristien Kemmer later even told me formally,

"I'm sorry, Billie Jean, but I can't hang around with you anymore. You get too much attention." Certainly, it is revealing that in the spring of 1975, right after I announced that I would be retiring from singles play after Wimbledon, Chris suddenly became much more friendly with me. She knew I'd be leaving the courts soon, so socializing would be more permissible now. I remember at a tournament down in Sarasota we spent the whole week together, like a couple of bobby-soxers, talking and laughing and polishing off hot fudge sundaes. There was some seriousness, too. She admitted to me then how she could understand why I would get an abortion. For a little Catholic girl of her upbringing, that was quite a statement.

Earlier, the previous fall, she had come to me when she was thinking about ending her engagement with Jimmy Connors. I certainly wouldn't characterize this as anything like Chris seeking me out for my advice. It was more on the order of her just needing someone older to listen to her. "Do you love Jimmy?" I asked.

"Oh, no, it isn't a question of love," Chris said. "I do love Jimmy. But I just don't know whether we should get married." And then she went on to tell me how much tennis meant to her, how much she wanted to be number one, and how she was terribly afraid that marriage could jeopardize that goal, because they were both so young and so competitive and they would have to be playing different schedules. Could they be champions and husbands and wives, too, successfully? It was very heavy; she was really tormented by the decision. I remember at one point in the conversation I tried to lighten things up by saying something funny, because Chris does have such a good sense of humor, but she wasn't interested. Not at all, not this day.

Fans only see a couple of famous athletes having a romance in the newspapers, but what Chris went through was a very traumatic time. She's a good Catholic, and Jimmy, too, and she wanted so much to have a marriage and a family, and it was terribly baffling to her when she realized the conflict that all these dreams posed with her tennis. It was even harder, in a way, because tennis was part of her upbringing, in the family, and so everything in her world was being pitted against itself.

I think it has always bugged Chris more than she lets on, too, that she has succeeded so as an athlete without having great raw physical talent. I doubt whether she—or Tracy, either, for that matter—could have been champions in any other sports. They both were programmed for tennis by their families, and they had a champion's temperament, perseverance, and concentration. Why, I saw Tracy hitting tennis balls when she was four years old, and she had perfect form—my eyes were out on stems.

And I'll tell you, as cool as Chris is, there's one thing she'll bite on every time. If I say to her, "Gee, that was really athletic what you did out there today," she'll light up right away and beam. "You think so?" she'll say, so proud, and then she'll finally catch on that I'm putting her on—again—and she'll get so angry at herself for taking the bait.

Chris loves that limelight a lot more than she lets on, too. Keep in mind that she was the first tennis player—of either sex—to have a tremendous amount of publicity right from the start. Everything she has done has been *historic*, and so, not surprisingly, she's come to think of attention as her natural due. It broke me up, at Wimbledon in 1981, after she had played a couple of dull early-round matches that didn't attract much in the way of a press-conference mob. She was really ticked off. She told me that if the Fourth Estate didn't get its act together and start appearing to listen to her in larger numbers, that she was just going to stop going to the interview room. "It's just no fun this way," Chrissie said.

You see, more than anything, Chris is a star. Some champions are simply winners; some are heroes; some are leaders.

Above all, though, Chris has been a star. In fact, she's the best star tennis ever had. None of the men have ever been a star like Chris, and no other of the women. Not really. But the other possible roles have not interested her. She is so single-minded. I've always thought that it was important for a players' union to be led by the best and most visible players, and with me more or less stirring things up—I worked on her for a year and a half—we elected Chris president of the WTA several years ago. But it never really flew. She wasn't comfortable in that position.

In my own mind, I'm confident that were it not for Chris we would now be holding the United States Women's Open at the Meadowlands in New Jersey instead of being part of the United States Open in Flushing Meadow. Better than 75 percent of the WTA wanted to make the move, but Chris stuck by the USLTA, and Tracy followed her lead. Without those two, we would have been crazy to make the move, and we didn't, even though we had a network deal set, we had sponsors ready to stick with us for several years, and we had a larger purse structure and a chance to make a percentage of future profits. Plus, above all, we would have our own identity. But Chris didn't want to chance it. She wanted to make some more points with the establishment. Besides, if there wasn't a USLTA–sanctioned United States championship to play for, how could Chris ever catch Helen Wills Moody's seven U.S. championships?

But so what is new? Chrissie and I have always been on different sides of that fence. She's not the villain, and neither should we even be in conflict. We shouldn't have to be even thinking about leaving Flushing Meadow, and neither should the men be happy at the prospect that we might be going. The trouble is, as ever, that the players fight too much against each other and not enough against the real enemy.

Part of the problem is that, a decade ago, I was too successful in helping obtain parity in prize money for the women. This was important at the time, but, looking back, I can see that it was a Pyrrhic victory. I helped the federations to turn the men more against us—divide and conquer—and made it easier for the major tournaments and the tennis-federation establishment to keep us down. What difference does it really make if the women earn as much as the men, but if both sexes are underpaid? The major tournaments, like the U.S. Open, like Wimbledon, rip the players off terribly.

Most of the run-of-the-mill weekly tournaments have to put up 40 percent of their gross in prize money. The majors offer no more than 10 percent, and perhaps as little as 6 or 8 percent. But of course, as long as the men and the women are at each others' throats, nobody is calling the major tournaments to a fair accounting, and they keep on raking it in.

It doesn't matter how much Chrissie and I might disagree on issues, because the game, its history, connects us. She understands that now, as well as I have. She came to me not long ago, and she said, "You know, Billie Jean, I finally understand what you felt like when I was growing up." The reference was to Tracy. I had my Chrissie, she has her Tracy; there's always a younger gunslinger somewhere. Austin has moved ahead of her now, eight wins to six as of December 1981, just as Chris eventually wore down my lead and finished ahead of me in our series.

At Toronto in 1981, when I saw Tracy beat Chris, trounce her, whip her at her own game, I felt so very sorry for Chris. I would have felt sorry for Tracy, for anybody, to have lost so decisively, but this was different. In a way, I can look at it all from such a distance now. My knees don't hurt. I'm not all hot and sweaty. I'm not on the line. But sometimes I can't completely disassociate myself—not when Chris is playing, anyway. I'll never feel for any of the others the way I do for her. It'll always seem a little more painful when she loses, for she became some part of me on the court, and no matter who won, each of us needed the other, because you're more of a player, not just for winning, but for beating someone special. And we always understood that, both of us.

■ ■ ■

Not long after she became established, Chris started making the point in interviews about how she and Evonne had finally come along, at last providing some femininity for women's tennis. I mean, it made it sound as if every one of us who had ever come before her had been some kind of witch. I bitched nicely a couple of times to her—"Hey, thanks a lot, Chris, I really needed that"—and she apologized and said she really didn't mean it that way, but she keeps on making the point, regularly.

Chris has always possessed a certain self-consciousness about being a sweaty old jock, and so heightening the perception of her absolute femininity is important to her. And I sympathize with her, with all of us, in this respect. Female athletes are stereotyped by the general population—and usually as homosexuals. And that is our bond. No, not that we are homosexuals, but that we are stereotyped. The reason that someone like Chris came to my defense when the Barnett affair became public was not because such a display of loyalty was good public relations and the best self-interest, but because all female athletes feel that we are treated unfairly in this regard by the public.

In a curious way, the straights were more upset and more defensive that the subject of homosexuality was being aired than were the gays. The straights understood that this would only make more people look askance at them. The gays had a more visceral reaction, but probably not for the reasons that you would imagine. It was not the disclosure of homosexuality per se that upset them. What was more disturbing to them was the overriding fact of Marilyn's betrayal. As lesbians, they live in a constant fear of being revealed, or of being blackballed in some way, and it was that element in the episode that most distressed them.

Now, very quickly I must hasten to insert here that I cannot speak as any sort of omniscient authority in these matters.

One of the more ridiculous results of this whole matter has been the widespread assumption that now, somehow, I am fully aware of and easily conversant with the sexual preferences of every woman tennis player—and, for that matter, of every female athlete. Why, you might just as well expect my brother, whose whole major-league career has been spent with the San Francisco Giants, to speak knowledgeably about the sex lives of the Baltimore Orioles—and the New England Patriots and Montreal Canadiens, too. Besides, what do I know? I'd always heard that all the lesbians were in the fashion world—right?

Probably, as a matter of fact, I've been less privy even to gossip about sex recently than anyone else. Given the circumstances, it is not exactly a subject the other players rush to bring up in my presence. I had to keep my eyes open. I had to laugh to myself when I noticed, for example, that one of the more prominent players, who I have always understood to be bisexual, suddenly started avoiding the locker room and took up again, very visibly, with an old boyfriend.

And some of the other response from the players was especially warm and funny. Shortly after the news broke, when I walked into the locker room at Surbiton, in England, a bunch of the black players all started screaming, "Get the showers going! Let's take our clothes off and all get in together!" Then Andrea Buchanan rushed over to where I was standing there laughing, put an arm around my shoulder, and said, "Come on, honey, let's go right out to the middle of the court and start kissing each other and really get everybody excited." (Poor, wonderful Andrea—she was killed by a robber a few months later.)

At Wimbledon the players were especially angered at a couple of minor fringe players who had taken money from the London scandal press to make outlandish statements about lesbianism in tennis. The *National Enquirer* had been offering money in the States, too, but not a single player of any consequence would take a nickel from that awful rag. In

London, when one of the Judases who had agreed to talk for a price came into the locker room, JoAnne Russell and Sherry Acker really let her have it. "Come on, girls," JoAnne said, "let's all of us pair up with our regulars and take our baths together." The player was so rattled she went into a toilet stall and wouldn't come out.

The New York *Post,* another scandal sheet, tried to get support for a ridiculous story which suggested that the parents of many young players were frightened to let their daughters go on tour because the old lesbian predators were stalking the kids in the showers. Tracy Austin, it was actually written, had a shower bodyguard. I trust that was so ridiculous that no one could even consider believing it, and, naturally, Jeanne Austin denied the rumor vehemently. The Jaegers also helped, because Andrea was my doubles partner in Japan at the next tournament on the schedule after my press conference, and when I offered to withdraw so that Andrea could not be embarrassed in any way, the Jaegers declared publicly that Andrea and all of her family were friends of mine and they would be proud to have her playing with me at any time. That sort of support made me feel so wonderful.

So much was blown out of proportion. I can only tell you that, from all my years in the sport, from everything I know, reports of the incidence of homosexuality are, like Mark Twain's death, greatly exaggerated. Even more important, perhaps, is the fact that among players themselves the subject is not a dominant one, and we are hardly divided into camps. Very few of all those supposed tour experts could discern who is what, anyway. The misconceptions are so great. For a while, I had a male secretary traveling with me on tour, and one night I was with him when a lot of the players all lined up in some sort of doubles presentation, and I asked Ron to tell me what he knew—who were the gays and who the straights. And he got it all wrong. I mean, he'd been on tour for months, he was an insider, and he was substantially in error.

On tour, you'll see the gays and the straights and the bis all hanging out together, going out for dinner. Doubles teams can often be made up of girls with different sexual preferences. And yet I have so often heard whispers about women becoming a doubles team because they were lesbians. Of course, I've never in my life heard any rumors about any male doubles partners being gay. Oh, no; in the male press, it's fraternity time. In the same way, as soon as one older woman starts coaching a younger player, the innuendo begins. But there is never any similar suggestion about an older male and his protégé. For that matter, you never hear any gossip when a young woman pro has an older male coach. You know how it is: if anything was going on, the press would wink at it and personally give the coach credit for his success with his student off the court, too.

Remember, too, that a woman athlete's personal life is always under such additional scrutiny. It isn't just the gays who are looking over their shoulder. To be a female athlete and have any kind of an affair is so much more emotionally wearing than what a male athlete must go through in a comparable situation. If one of us is seen having dinner with a strange man on the road, we're obviously trash, a roundheels, while the male athlete with a dinner date is a smoothy, a Don Juan; boys will be boys. In my own special case, I am twice guilty—not only for having had a homosexual affair, but for being a cheating wife. As a matter of fact, on the marital-sin scale of what is generally accepted in America, I did everything wrong. The least sinful sex escapade is for a man on the road to have a one-nighter with a member of the opposite sex that he treats strictly as a throwaway object. That's just one step up from not getting your library book back on time. But me? I'm the worst because I'm a woman who had a caring, extended affair with a member of the same sex near home.

Whereas male athletes are celebrated so in our society, female athletes are hardly treated with the same honor. The Women Sports Foundation has done so much educational work in helping to correct this situation—and the greater money and attention that female athletes are receiving now hasn't hurt, either. Still, we are short of full acceptance.

As a consequence, and especially in years past, we players have probably turned within, to the safe haven of the tour. It was family, but almost exclusively an all-female family, and no doubt that made many of us more female-oriented—and I don't necessarily mean in a sexual way. But now, as I've said, we have more general acceptance, and even if women pros stay close to the tour, it is no longer the small club it used to be. There are people of both sexes and all ages along now. Ours will be a more normal world, more representative of the general population in many ways.

Women sports professionals also operate at a tremendous disadvantage when we are compared to the other types of young women who have historically been in the spotlight. Always before, women on view have been expected to appear exceptionally beautiful. Indeed, more often than not, the main reason why a woman was selected to be in the spotlight was because she was good-looking. Men and women alike thus came to be culturally programmed to expect to see only beautiful young women on public view.

We, as athletes, simply don't measure up to these traditional expectations. We can't cover our bodies—particularly our imperfections—nor can we wear any kind of falsies; our makeup quickly disappears, and yet we have to appear nearly naked out there. We're sweating, our hair is all quickly askew, and we don't have thirty-seven takes under ideal lighting conditions to get it just right. I'm quite sure, given this situation, that most of the women in the world would be dismissed as queers and freaks if they had to appear in the culturally prejudiced manner that we must.

It takes a lot of courage for a woman to be an athlete on

display. Worse, if you win—which is, after all, the point—
then you know there is a tendency for many people to devalue
your success for physical reasons. To this day, and despite all
contradictory evidence, there remains the widespread opinion that an unattractive woman will make a better athlete
than an attractive one, because she has diminished opportunities elsewhere in a sexist world and thus will be hungrier in
sports.

I mentioned earlier that the first person in tennis to tell me
I'd be champion was Frank Brennan, a man I've always liked
and admired. But shortly after he "discovered" me, he told
me flat-out why I had a special reason to do well. "You'll be
good because you're ugly, Billie Jean," he said. Just like that.
And he didn't believe that he was being mean. He made that
remark in the same way as he might say, "You'll be good
because you have a nice backhand, Billie Jean."

But I was sixteen years old then, and while that would be
painful to hear any day of your life, you can imagine what it
did to me at the time. I was devastated.

In so many ways, too, we're damned if we do, damned if we
don't. If we're athletic, we're mannish. We're alleged to be
aggressive broads, and any real competitive fire we exhibit is
antifeminine. Male athletes are expected to grab each other,
jump in each other's arms, hug, tousle each other's hair, slap
each other on the bahoola, rejoice with each other; but if
women athletes show anything more than a handshake for
one another, that's further proof that they're all three-dollar
bills.

It's not easy to know what you're supposed to do in this
country, is it? When I grew up, as in most households, I, the
girl, would kiss both my parents, but my brother would only
kiss Mom. Pointedly, he and Dad would shake hands. Now, as
a baseball player, he can pat other male players on the rear,
but can you imagine the reaction if I, a tennis player, patted
Chrissie that way after we won a big doubles match? You
need a scorecard to keep all the double standards straight.

But there are some absolutes. In all my years on the tour, I was never, in even the remotest possible manner, approached by another player for sexual reasons. The lesbians I know would never think of proselyting younger players, in a shower or anywhere else. In fact, the only case like that I can ever remember was when a young player, just on tour, went after an older one, and the older woman was so stunned and bemused by the whole business that she lost her composure. It was almost hilarious. Where are those bodyguards when we need them?

I am not, however, suggesting that the subject of lesbianism never even comes up. It has always been a background murmur. It was first brought to my attention back when I came on the old amateur tour and somebody quietly advised me, just to keep me posted, that two of the older players were enjoying a long-standing affair. Coming from my middle-class naiveté, I was somewhat fascinated by this worldly revelation, but it pretty much quickly faded from my mind. It's a good thing I was filled in, though, because otherwise I never would have known. The two women acted perfectly normal in their behavior, they were discreet together, and neither one ever approached another player. In fact, they both seemed better adjusted than a lot of the other players, and when they left tennis they went their separate ways, and one of them subsequently got married.

Then, too, on a couple of occasions in the WTA councils, the subject of lesbianism has come up—but only from the point of view of the public perception. Stereotyping. Once, I remember, one of the officers shook her head and then laughed that she would put a motion on the floor that "every WTA member must bring a boyfriend to the WTA dinner." And neck with him in public.

There have also been occasions when I've participated in personal conversations with gays. I remember an especially touching one, where my friend told me, "Hey, I don't like being this way, but it's just the way I am, and it's the way I've always been, and I can't do anything about it." But I have also had personal conversations with other players about their boyfriends and their marriages and their families and a variety of other subjects.

Take Martina Navratilova, for example. It has been tough for her being stateless, turning her back on the culture and country of her childhood, yearning to be accepted—formally and otherwise—by the land she wants to be part of. None of us really know how much her inconsistency in playing has been related to difficulties in her personal life.

She is so very bright in so many ways, with a wonderfully facile mind. She picks up languages with incredible ease; she can master any sort of word game or numbers game; there isn't a point she ever played that she cannot punch back up on her computer mind. But like a lot of people of that nature, Martina seems to possess a weak grasp on the everyday fundamentals of life; she is not a superstar in the common-sense league. She does some things without realizing how she may be hurting someone. I don't mean that she's intentionally cruel; she just doesn't think.

For example, when she decided to junk me as her doubles partner in 1980 so that she could team up with Pam Shriver, Martina just went ahead and did it. I mean, she never said a word to me; the woman is the last to know—right? Months went by, and never an explanation, an apology—nothing. Finally one time I couldn't stand it any longer, and I screamed at her, "You at least owe me this much—say something!" But she just walked right past me. "Come on, Martina," I yelled after her, "tell me I'm too old, tell me I can't play anymore, tell me I'm a gimp—anything—but *tell me something.*" But even that outburst didn't do any good. Martina just kept right on walking because she didn't want to face up to anything unpleasant.

On the court, Martina's problem is that she's convinced

that she's a superduperstar (and she could be), but until recently she hasn't wanted to pay the price to win. She's also been too mopey and has projected the wrong image to be a gate attraction, and that irritates her all the more, that she is not popular. You see, all along, Martina hasn't just wanted to become an American. More than that, she's wanted all of America to love her.

In the same way, I've often doubted that Martina cared all that much for tennis. Instead, I think that she primarily loves what tennis will bring her. It doesn't matter what it is, so long as it is an acquisition.

Quite honestly, until August 1981, when she finally began to think about the game, and to start getting herself back in shape again, I thought Martina was going backward. I thought the chances of her ever winning another major title were remote. In my opinion, her serve had deteriorated badly, she had failed to improve her footwork, and she couldn't be bothered with learning how to come over her backhand and turn it into an offensive shot. But, you see, she could get by. She is such a fine athlete and so powerful that she could always stay in the top five or six just on the basis of her natural ability.

She needs someone to drive her. In 1978, the year she really started to win, Sandra Haynie was her manager, really directing Martina. I had a bad foot, so I started helping Sandra, working on Martina's endurance, forcing her to go all out, keeping her pulse up for twenty minutes at a clip. That's the only way you'll ever develop stamina. I kept telling her, too, that when things go wrong, don't moan and slump and slink around. Instead, use adversity to get your gumption up and fight back. Soon Martina was clearly number one in the world, but after she won her second Wimbledon in a row in 1979, she began to slack off, and not till late in the summer of '81 did she draw herself together again.

Still, at this point, it remains difficult for me to tell how determined she will stay. Martina is not unlike another great, strong athlete, Margaret Court, both of them front-runners who could too often come up short in a showdown. That is the way Martina played against Tracy in the final at the U.S. Open in 1981. She won the first set 6–1, but then lost two tiebreakers, when she could never quite finish things off. It is only more recently that Martina seems to have added those last touches of the right emotional gloss to her physical game.

16 TWO RULES AND OTHER TRUTHS

The funny thing is, when I was starting out, I never thought of myself in terms of *women's* tennis. It was all just tennis to me. The media put me into women's tennis. Of course, I would have to say that I surely would have found my way there on my own, because I discovered quickly enough where women were supposed to always be in tennis—the warm-up match, the prelim, the undercard.

That was especially frustrating because in this country we really do have the most enlightened approach to women. But as I discovered, when it comes to female athletes, and particularly on a personal basis, older American men are the worst, the absolute chauvs of the world. The Aussies are the ones who are supposed to be so antifemale. Every woman is a "Sheilah," someone who is supposed to sit over in the corner with the other Sheilahs until you've had enough beers with the boys and want some quick sex. But for all that, the Aussies were always good about practicing with the women players and helping us out.

It's tough for a girl to ask a boy to hit with her; it's even more of an imposition than asking him out on a date, and I always tried to avoid it. But the few times I made myself do it, if the guy I asked was American, the experience was sure to be a horrible one. I remember one time with Stan Smith, Mr. Nice Guy, at The Queen's Club, and there was nobody left but each other, we had to practice together, and even though we were out there together for no more than a half an hour, Stan made it obvious to me that he thought the whole business was a total waste for him. The American men—especially the older generations—so often have that superior attitude. When I traveled with all the Aussie guys in the National Tennis League, the worst thing they could say about a countryman was "He's getting too American." Of a Yank they didn't like, they would say, "He thinks the sun shines out of his ass."

Of course, many of the Aussies ended up immigrating here, so I guess they couldn't have thought that America was all bad. And you can be sure the Aussies were accepted. America is the one place where it rarely makes any difference where the sports stars come from. Americans just want to see the best. Well, there are some exceptions. I agreed with World Team Tennis a few years ago that the best place for me to play would be in New York. But we were dead wrong.

New York is such an aggressive place, so that it's best to be a male athlete there—or male anything, I suppose. New York is also a hang-out city, and of course the last thing I'm interested in are the right bars and restaurants. It would have been wiser for World Team Tennis to have had a Broadway Jane starring for the Apples instead of a stay-at-home like me, even if I was then the biggest name on the courts.

Women tennis players really do appreciate the male players who give us a fair shake. Sandy Mayer, for example, was the best of all the Americans at practicing with us. And—

surprise!—I'll mention another who wasn't so bad about that: Pancho Gonzales. He could pick on any female he thought was getting "uppity," but if he knew that you cared about the game, he never had any qualms about working out with a woman. On tour, he and Frankie Durr were a real odd couple, because they'd be out there on the practice court almost every afternoon, hitting until it became too dark to see.

But the one American player almost universally admired by the women pros—even if almost none of them know him at all well personally—is Jimmy Connors. He can be vulgar out there on the court and sometimes act the fool, but Jimmy always gives so much of himself, and this is what the women love him for. I know I do, and I'll bet there are more women players on the tour who try and emulate Connors's spirit than any other male player.

It was typical, a few years ago, when he was struggling against Adriano Panatta at Flushing Meadow, in the U.S. Open. The crowd, as always, was for him, and all the more so as he fought to get back in the match. The fans give Jimmy a lot, and he gives that back to them. That's why I love the way he is. And I was there, down near the court, and I was screaming for him as loudly as anyone, and he saw me and would yell back at me. Jimmy did win the match, and then, later, he made a point to seek me out. "Thanks for being there and cheering for me," he said.

Personally, I think I've always understood why players like Connors act the way they do on the court, because I've always been a volatile, temperamental player myself. In fact, when Elton John wrote the song "Philadelphia Freedom" for me, he told me that the beat came from his perception of how I stomped around the court. I can still see him now, bringing the rough mix of the song on a cassette, playing it, and stomping around in imitation of me in this filthy World Team Tennis locker room we had to use in Denver. But then, I must have a pretty good stomp when I'm angry because that beat carried "Philadelphia Freedom" to number one on the charts.

People want to know why I can't always control myself—or why Connors and McEnroe can't. The problem is that we all have something of a split personality, and I always fear that if I give in to one side—that nice, polite me—then I'll stop caring about victory, and my sweet indifference will defeat me. Now, maybe that sounds ridiculous, but keep in mind that athletes tank for the same babyish reasons. Subconsciously you say to yourself, All right, I'll be a good sport, but I can't be a winning player if I have to concentrate on my behavior so.

If there is one thing about Connors where I disagree with him, it is that he has been too narrow in his accomplishments, almost skipping doubles altogether. This applies even more so to Borg. I don't see how he can be satisfied with his achievement and think of himself as an exceptionally great player without seeking success in every phase of the game. I give McEnroe so much more credit for winning at singles and doubles alike. For me, I am proudest that I not only won major titles on all surfaces, but also that in the doubles championships I won, I played both right and left court, and both about an equal number of times. At different times I even won Wimbledon in both the ad and the deuce court with the same partner, Rosie Casals. That's what I'm proudest of, that I did it all.

The men tend to be more rigid in their thinking about the game. It was considerably more difficult to get them to try World Team Tennis, which has always amused me because it was in 1976, his one season of WTT, that Borg learned to chip and come in. He probably wouldn't agree with me, but that's where I think he became a fast-court player, where he gained the tools which made it possible for him to win his first Wimbledon. And two years before that, although Ken Rosewall never stopped complaining about Team Tennis, he got his game back; that was the summer, out of nowhere, when he got to the finals of both Wimbledon and Forest Hills.

In the same way that so many of the top men, like Borg and Connors, refuse to play doubles, rarely will you ever find a good male player who will deign to play mixed. And for those men anywhere who do play mixed—Nastase is the one exception—they are convinced that it is written in stone that the male must play the left court. That is where the dominant partner is supposed to be. Teddy Tinling is always saying that to me when I play women's doubles: "But Madame Superstar, you must play the left. Your personality demands it."

But it is one of the great myths in tennis that the stronger player must line up in the left court. Just consider this: the right-court player is, in every set, going to get a few more points to play. And, unless he or she is left-handed, you should have the better returner in the right court. Perhaps the very toughest shot in mixed doubles is the wide slice serve, which (assuming a right-handed server) will come into the forehand court. A man, with his greater reach and power, is the logical one to play that shot back. (The closest thing to a universal law in tennis is: never put a lefty in the forehand court, where the southpaw would have to try and return wide slices with a backhand. Left-handers have a difficult time hitting backhands crosscourt, while their best shot is the opposite: a forehand, hooked crosscourt. So, no matter what other factors are involved, including gender or ability, you're almost always wisest to play the left-hander in the left court.)

Of course, I've always thought, too, that even though the assumption has become accepted that the dominant man must play the left side, the right side is really the more difficult half to play. Oh, yes. On the right, you don't have so much a feeling of space, and few players ever learn to hit what I call the "off" backhand, that little inside-out backhand that you need to hit from in the middle of the court off the right side. Curiously, for some reason that shot always came naturally for me.

A lot of the left-right court stuff is psychological, too. While it is true, for example, that the left-court player is going to be faced with more points that actually decide a game, that does not mean that he or she will necessarily play more crucial points. The right-court player can't just bang away every time at deuce, figuring, So what if I lose this, there's still my partner to bail us out. If you're a right-court player, you must get a high percentage of returns in play; you cannot let your partner constantly be getting the serve at a disadvantage. I don't know if any other player but me ever did this, but what I often did was fantasize in the right court. If it was deuce, for example, I would tell myself that it was really 40–15 against us, that I absolutely *had* to win the point to keep us in the game.

In fact, singles or doubles, there are many instances when the key point is not the break point itself. Any dunce can cry out "Break point" whenever one pops up, but the fact is that often the climax of a game or a set or even a match has occurred before most fans—and a lot of players—have realized it. Again, it's easy to say that the champions play well on the big points, but that is only part of it. I think champions have almost an innate feeling, an instinct, for appreciating what, in fact, the big points are.

The dominant player on a doubles team must also possess a feel about how much of the upper hand to exert. This is especially true in mixed. Obviously, the male player should be in command, but he must also be sure only to exert a selective dominance. The man who forces his partner out of position or who forces bad shots that the woman is better lincd up for is just digging a grave for them both. Look, I'm not dumb, I know what my mixed partners said about me behind my back: Let Billie Jean think she's the one in charge, give her a few extra shots to keep her happy. That sort of thing. But the fact is, if the woman is not involved in the rallies, it is going to be that much more difficult for her to exert herself when she is suddenly obliged to at an important moment in the match.

At least for now, too, men should have a better sense of how to operate out there as a doubles *team*, because male athletes have had so much more training in the team sports. I think one reason why I managed so well in doubles is that I had the instincts of team play better than most women, and even if I never played on any organized team. A lot of women simply don't have a clue how to fit in, how to fill a role—all the sort of thing that comes with playing as part of a team. Owen Davidson used to say that he always felt like he was playing men's doubles with me.

For me, possibly my supreme doubles accomplishment was in the Wightman Cup of 1970, which was played at Wimbledon, when Peaches Bartkowicz and I had to play Virginia Wade and Winnie Shaw in the final match. The Cup was tied at three matches apiece, and not only were the British a good team, but they were playing before the home crowd—and Peaches was not exactly a classic doubles type.

She was like Chris, only worse, because she just couldn't stand ever to go to the net. But she had a great return of serve and outstanding groundies, so I sorted this situation out, and I told her, "Look, don't even worry about coming to the net. We'll play it this way: you take it back, and I'll take it up." And we did. We played the absolute worst way you can set up for doubles, one up and one back, but it was a surprise team improvisation, and it snuck us through in three sets, and we won the Cup.

Understand, I'm not saying that men naturally make better team players than women do. It is just that we haven't had the team training they have. We're never as detached as we should be when it comes to breaking up a team. I mentioned, for example, how Martina couldn't even face me when she decided to set up a new shop with Pam Shriver. And Rosie was distraught several years ago when I told her I thought the time had come for us to split. But we had been together too long—seven or eight years, playing constantly—and we were growing stale together. The reason why I thought we should call it a day on the court was because we'd both do better with new tennis partners, but our friendship wouldn't deteriorate any more, along with our doubles game.

The fact is, too, that as tennis becomes more of a spectator attraction, doubles is going to play more of a role. This is no wild-eyed prediction, but a rational projection, simply because more of the spectators play doubles themselves and a doubles match is usually a better show. Because there are more variables in doubles, it can be handicapped more efficiently and there is less of a likelihood for one-sided matches. Doubles has more upsets. It's a better entertainment buy.

And as doubles picks up, so is mixed bound to gain in popularity. Much of what has been holding it back is that nobody, with the exception of Team Tennis, has been supporting mixed. Even now, at the big tournaments, a lot of the players—of both sexes—who enter the mixed really only do so in order to get extra tickets.

But the fact is that mixed doubles has obvious sex appeal— for both sexes—and it is bound to become more competitive as the females improve relatively more than the males. In the years ahead, we are bound to have a steeper graph of development. Already we know there is not that much difference between what the top male and female athletes can achieve with their legs. Whether we are talking about skiing, skating, or running, short or long distances, men are only about 10 or 15 percent faster than women. In many swimming events women are compiling better records than what men were achieving only a generation ago. Male Olympic champions of 1960 would not, with their times, have won medals swimming against women in the 1980 Olympics. And keep in mind that this development spans my playing career. What can happen in the years immediately ahead, and especially as athletics finds more cultural acceptance among women?

There does remain a great deal of differential in the upper-body strength of the two sexes, so that men can still hit or throw a ball much harder, but even this is not necessarily an eternal verity. When men and women alike have had their nondominant arms tested—the left arms of right-handers— the difference has been slight; both sexes appear spasto. I'm not spouting any Amazon supersex claims. The serious point is that women's athletic potential has not been developed nearly so much as men's, and so we are almost surely going to close the gap in the years ahead.

It is also to our advantage as tennis players—although I take no great comfort in this—that tennis is *the* sport for women today. There are no exceptionally popular team sports, such as soccer or baseball, to steal the best female athletes away from tennis. I have often said that women's sports will have arrived *only* when women's team sports are accepted, but until then women's tennis will have a much larger pool of talent to draw from than will men's. The fact that more financial support is being directed toward women's athletics, and the fact that a female athlete can now make a viable, even handsome, living, will also attract more young women into the field. Sports will become a vehicle for upward mobility for girls in the same way as it has traditionally been one for boys. And there are whole unenlightened parts of the world where men's athletics have thrived but where women's have never so much as been tolerated, and this attitude is bound to fade with time. Potentially, there are so many women in this world who may turn more to sports, to tennis. The great gender gap will be narrowed. Bet on that.

Certainly, too, as we women attract better athletes to our game, we're going to get fewer of the backcourt machines and more all-court players. We need that now. But I don't ever want to see the Austins and the Evert Lloyds disappear, because the ideal spectator match features variety: the puncher versus the counterpuncher. That is true whether you're talking about two women trading groundstrokes from the baseline or two men trading serve-and-volley.

Naturally, I am prejudiced. I'm proud of having been an attacking player—especially because I believe that that breed is always out there taking more of a risk. When you're an attacking player you're dealing with a smaller margin of error, you're more prone to be distracted, you're living on the precipice. I think the fans recognize this and are prepared to give you the benefit of the doubt. Probably attacking players are naturally more exuberant, too. Net players are usually tall, with nice long legs, like Shriver and Kathy Jordan now, and that sure doesn't hurt, either, does it? You know, when all is said and done, I think that my greatest accomplishment of all may be that I'm the only champion who ever played a net game who was under five feet seven. And I'm almost three inches under.

In the complete overall history of tennis, I figure I'll be worth a sentence or two. Well, maybe a paragraph, counting the Riggs match. That's why my place in the all-time rankings means so very little to me, because I know I won't be anybody's number one, and it's that same old thing: if you're not number one, then what does it really matter?

My problem, anyway, was always that I was so dependent on who I was playing. It wasn't very often that I beat people love and one, as I took Evonne in my last Wimbledon final. If somebody was playing well, I could be carried along. If my opponent was playing badly, I tended to drift down toward her level. I was a match player.

You know the best match I ever saw? It was one between Rod Laver and Tony Roche. I remember it was played in Brisbane, but I can't remember what tournament or what round. It was just two players at their very best. It was about a hundred and ten degrees on the court, and they went five sets, and I'll bet there weren't three hundred people—tops— watching. But it was incredible tennis. Laver won in five sets. He usually did. Poor Tony; he never believed in himself. If he'd had Newcombe's ego to go with his game, he'd never have been beaten.

But you see, that's what upsets me so about the fuss they make over Borg's accomplishments, the five straight Wimbledons. It isn't his fault, I know, that he is given such credit, but it irritates me that so many great players who preceded him—Budge and Gonzales and Laver, even my old pal Kramer—simply didn't have the same opportunity. As soon as they turned pro they were locked out of Wimbledon. How many straight years could some of them have won? Look at Laver. Rod won in '61 and '62 as an amateur, then again in '68 and '69 as soon as Wimbledon went open. Who wouldn't say that he would have won all the years in between too— nine straight, all told?

Clay-court tennis is a special abomination. I won on the clay; I have my French. But even when I won, it was too slow and it wasn't good entertainment. At last I've even gotten Chrissie to admit that. "Well, yeah, you're right, Billie Jean," she said. And then she quickly smiled and added, "But I still like it because I win on it." I don't care; quality should always be able to trump mere perseverance. If an endurance contest is your pleasure, go watch Channel swimming.

Whatever the surface, old-timers bug me by maintaining that the tiebreaker has rendered conditioning much less important. But that's just not so. Assuming players are in fairly good shape, it isn't conditioning that will necessarily do them in in a long match. The problem is adrenaline because it is so hard to get it flowing again. That's why the player who goes through a long, close match so often has a letdown in the next round and is eliminated. But on most occasions, it was not a question of fitness, as everyone assumes.

The fact is that the players today are in better shape than players have ever been. Nobody smokes—absolutely no one— and in all my years on tour, I never met a player with a drinking problem. What alcohol is consumed is almost always beer. The cheap newspapers are always trying to expose a drug culture on the tour, but it simply doesn't exist. Now, obviously, you are dealing with a lot of young people in their twenties, and they will, in many ways, mirror the society they live in when they're away from tennis. If young men or women in their twenties smoke pot or whatever, you're going to get some of that from some tennis players. And probably, at any particular time, it is possible to find a good player or two, male and female, who are messing around with something heavier. I've seen a couple players of both sexes blowing their noses regularly into a towel, and I've seen blood on the towel, and I've seen these players play a great first set and then stumble, just as if they were crashing off a high. So I'm not naive. There must be some cocaine going around—and some good players may use it sometimes. But it is surely no epidemic.

Another reason why players are in so much better shape today is because the care and treatment is considerably improved. I say this, too, while also noting that sports medicine still remains primitive in many respects. Even for these incredibly healthy young specimens, doctors will almost reflexively prescribe pills instead of suggesting exercise or some other form of therapy. But still, when I first started playing, we didn't even know whether it was proper to put ice on an injury. If, for example, I had known about the kind of weight training that my wonderful friend the late Dr. John Marshall had Pam Shriver use for her shoulder, there is no telling how much agony and recuperation I could have been spared.

Being hurt is so terrible. In a very real sense, I never was truly bothered when I lost if I was healthy. Even growing old is different from being hurt. At least when you're older you can still pretty much do everything—only not so well, not so hard, not so fast, not for so long. But injury deprives you, and that is different.

It's incredible, too, how much more advanced coaching has become in the last couple decades. When I learned, the procedure was for the player to bounce a ball and then swat at it. That, of course, is ridiculous; it's like learning to hit a slider in baseball by punching out fungoes. The way I was taught, I probably wouldn't be able to make it now. I learned my strokes too late in life. I only survived those first few years because I was quick and athletic. Even when I was fat, I had great lateral speed and I could jump. So that kept me in the game until I could learn to play the game. But a kid couldn't get by like that today.

I learned to hit a forehand improperly, and I never really could fully correct myself. That very first day I played, I started hitting with too closed a stance, and even when I was the best player in the world, I still had trouble hitting a ball in close to me with my forehand. It was five years before I understood that you should hit low to high, and by the time I did appreciate that, it was too late for me. It was almost another ten years before I saw that I was opening the face of the racket too much on my backswing for my forehand (which is, by the way, the exact opposite of what Connors also does with his short forehand, which is why he hits so many approaches into the net—because he starts fiddling with his stroke at the last moment in order to compensate).

You see, in the final analysis, so much of it is execution. That's what matters the most. All the stuff about psychology is overrated. Fans place entirely too much emphasis on players psyching one another. It's enough to get yourself organized and to pray that your opponent won't have a great day, without plotting how to con her. Ultimately, the whole game is determined in that microsecond when the racket makes contact with the ball. And it doesn't matter how you get there. Look at the three top men, for example. McEnroe has a short backswing, Connors comes far back, straight back, and Borg makes a loop, but they all hit it exactly the same—squared off at the point of contact, as in golf.

Intuition is also blown way out of proportion. I've always been able to keep in mind where I've been hitting my shots—

two backhands down the line off her forehands, then one crosscourt, that kind of stuff—and where my opponent has been hitting hers. And there are certain predictabilities you tend to assimilate. Almost everyone will tend to fade a low volley, but they'll hit a high one the other way across court. *Almost* everyone, that is; a few players, like Virginia Wade, for example, with a different grip, will hit those shots differently. But the point is, you study, you learn the probabilities and the personal exceptions, you put all that knowledge together, and you're liable to make an intelligent guess as to where to expect the return.

Sometimes I think you're wisest only to keep two rules in mind. The first one is the first one that Clyde Walker ever taught me, that first day I ever walked on the court. It is: Close the gate.

The second one is: The match is not over till you shake hands at the net.

At the Clairol Crown in 1980, I had Martina match point—*serving* for the match—5–4 in the second set, and I hit a nearly perfect first serve down the middle that she could hardly lay her racket on. She just barely managed to get the ball back, and I volleyed it right into the corner, but she was able to lunge and just reach the ball. It was a stab. In fact, it ticked the top of the net and flew up, and I was barely able to get my racket on it, and Martina banged my little return away. I didn't win another point in that set, and she beat me 6–0 in the third set.

The main thing is to care. Care very hard, even if it is only a game you are playing. The other day I found a letter I wrote to myself in 1975. I wrote it on hotel stationery as I traveled to London to try and win one last Wimbledon. And this is what I wrote to myself:

The clickety, clackety of the train wheels and the old English countryside passing by, and where have the last fifteen years gone?!? The sun is shining its warmth through the train window and that helps alleviate the pain I feel right now in my innermost self.

The reason for writing to myself with this lethal weapon is to show my thought process and put my mind in order. When there is this confusion, one must put aside some precious moments to experience *silencio* and attempt to find inner peace.

To stand on the Centre Court at Wimbledon, winning yet another singles title—but more important, my *last* major tournament singles match—is a hope that brings a vivid vision of tremendous joy and tears. I picture myself completely breaking down. Then the people would realize what life on Centre Court has meant through the last two-thirds of my entire life.

But more important now, I must think in terms of very specific goals and realities. Of course, I can just say I want to win all three—the singles, doubles, and mixed. Easy to say and easy to want, but so difficult to execute. How can I do it? More than anything else, I must *love* everything that is part and parcel of the total Wimbledon scene. I must love hitting that little white ball; love every strain of running and bending those tired knees; love every bead of sweat; love every cloud or every ray of sun in the sky; love every moment of tension, waiting in the locker room; love the lack of total rest every night, the hunger pains during the day, taking a bath in my favorite tub, buying lollies for the ball boys, looking at the ivy and the trees and the flower arrangements, driving through Roehampton on the way to the courts every morning, practicing on the outside court with your stomach in your throat before the match; love watching people queue, knowing some of them have waited twenty years to experience one day at Wimbledon; love playing on the Fourth of July, talking with Mrs. Twyman, having a rubdown, hearing the women talk (or not talk), and feeling the tension in the air, running up to the tea room through the crowds; love feeling and absorbing the tradition of almost one hundred years.

In essence, I have to possess enough passion and love to withstand all the odds. No matter how tough, no matter what kind of outside pressure, no matter how many bad breaks along the way, I must keep my sights on the final goal, to win, win, win—and with more love and passion than the world has ever witnessed in any performance. A total, *giving* performance: give more when you think you have nothing left. Through the desire the inspiration will be present. Love, passion, attitude, ability, intensity—the only way, a street with no curves or *cul-de-sacs*. I must let my inner self be out front and free. Love always.

17 VULNERABLE, AT LAST

I might have been a sweaty career woman (the worst kind, as far as a lot of people are concerned), but no matter how much some people may have hated me, I never felt a lack of respect. Never. That was one vibration I always had.

And you know, even after the affair came out, I still sense that respect. Still. Oh, I was scared at first. I just didn't want to be seen; I didn't want to be anywhere where people could look at me. When I did have to go out, I could feel the people staring at me, and you can imagine what went through my brain. Sometimes I could tell without a doubt that someone was looking at me harshly. At first I thought that was hatred I saw in their eyes, but as time went along I began to suspect that what was actually there was only fear and confusion. So I began to feel better.

As best I can tell, it's only been a small percentage of people who have reacted negatively against me—mostly that Moral

Majority crowd that loves to quote Jesus . . . selectively. In my case, for example, I haven't heard any of them say, "Judge not, that ye be not judged." And I sure don't want to generalize myself, either. During Team Tennis, just a few weeks after everything came out, we played one night in San Diego, which is real dyed-in-the-wool-Republican, Middle America mentality, and I was especially concerned about how they would react to me. You know what happened? When I was introduced, I got a long standing ovation. After that I knew that it wasn't any majority and certainly not a moral one that disapproved of me.

Mainly I was damaged financially. Illingworth-Morris was bringing out a tennis-clothing line by the name of Wimbledon, and I was the logical American to represent them as a spokesperson; they invited me to be just that, and the deal, which was 90 percent finalized, was canceled when the news broke, and that cost me $500,000. I also lost an existing contract with Murjani jeans—$300,000 gone. I lost a $45,000 deal with Charleston Hosiery, a $90,000 Japanese clothing contract, and my business managers estimate that, for the next three years, I lost $225,000 in various television commercials, $150,000 in corporate appearances, and $150,000 for coaching and training. That means, in a very conservative accounting, I lost almost $1,500,000 on account of Marilyn's suit and her lawyer.

Plus, it cost me an awful lot of money in lawyers' fees to get Marilyn out of my house and out of my life. I did feel a great deal of vindication when the judge, Julius M. Title, ruled so completely for us. It wasn't just that he ordered Marilyn out, either; it wasn't just that he found no merit in her case; it was that he went even further, saying that Marilyn exhibited "unconscionable conduct" and "really is not coming into a court of equity with clean hands."

Judge Title went on: "And I also have to be candid enough to say that I believe for Barnett now to contend that the letters were being retained by her for sentimental purposes under the facts and circumstances of this situation is just not credible. . . . I believe, and I find that when Barnett refused to proceed with that agreement and give up the letters and the house as well, there was an express or implied threat of adverse publicity . . . and it just appears to me to be clearly inferable from the evidence the reason she didn't go forward was because at that point she had decided that perhaps she could do better than the $125,000.

"If that isn't an attempted extortion, it certainly comes close to it."

Still, even hearing those words, even that most total and utter legal vindication, could not repair the damage done. Some wounds cannot be healed, no matter how good the doctors, how successful the operation.

The verdict was handed down only a couple of weeks before Christmas, so there was even more reason to be joyous. That evening we went to "victory" parties at both our lawyers' offices, and, curiously, I didn't share the feeling of elation that all the people who had worked on the case showed. In the sense of "victory," I was happy only for our lawyers, Dennis Wasser and Henry Holmes, and all their associates who had worked so hard on the case. They were wonderful. They deserved to win, for, no less than an athlete, they prepared and they got the job done. And truly, I know, whatever their egos, that Dennis and Henry had won *for* us, for Larry and me . . . but still, there was really no way that ever we could win.

Some people did stand by me, all along. NBC kept me as one of the Wimbledon announcers—even though we had not officially signed a contract at the time when things broke. NBC even went the extra mile, using me with Bud Collins as a commentator on some of the *men's* matches—the first time a woman had ever been used at a major tournament in that capacity. Yonex and Nike and Achilles and Power Grip also continued to use me for their products, but, of course, I have no illusions that, as my contracts run out, some sponsors may choose to quietly drop me. And will any new product ever dare to sign me?

It is difficult to accurately assess the situation, due to the fact that I was pretty much retiring from competitive big-time tennis. There has been a definite trend in America lately to hire retired, middle-aged male athletes for commercial endorsements. So possibly there may be some paydays which lie ahead. Of course, it is also true that when it comes to celebrity in America, middle-aged men are tolerated more than middle-aged women. Leading men are still playing love scenes in the movies long after their original leading ladies have been put out to pasture. Historically, too, more in the way of bland behavior is required of women who are hired by business to be in the public eye. As far back as 1893, a soap company fired an actress named Lillie Langtry from doing their advertisements when it became public knowledge that she was having an affair. Even though Ms. Langtry remained a great star, the soap people never used her again. Male celebrities often enhance their commercial value with controversy, but it certainly doesn't turn out that way with us working girls. Isn't it ironic how much Anita Bryant, with her outspoken criticism of homosexuality, and I share?

In any event, however much Marilyn and her lawyer have—and may yet—cost me in dollars and cents, I feel worse for how the public exposure has hurt the people who love me. In many ways my father is still in shock. I remember after the press conference, when we were getting on an elevator, and I had to just put my arms around him and hold him, he was shaking so. My poor mother has been even slower to come around.

Larry was punished personally and professionally. Two major sponsors dropped out of projects he was promoting, simply because he was my husband—and one of the deals had nothing whatsoever even to do with tennis. The sad part is, too, that Larry was just starting to really make it when this affair broke. Of course, as always, he's managed to take it in stride. "I've always been an anonymous person," he told one of our friends. "I've just lost a little of my anonymity, that's all." In fact, he lost much, much more. In simple dollars and cents, Larry lost some $400,000 at last count.

I've also been afraid that I would smear my women friends, merely by association. I remember being with Connie Spooner, the tennis trainer, at an airport shortly after the affair became public, and I felt compelled to suggest to her that she move away from me. For that matter, sometimes I've even felt that I would somehow be damaging the reputation of a man I was alone with, that people would think he had to be really strange to hang around with me. But perhaps the unfairest attention fell on Ilana Kloss, because she happened to be my doubles partner at the time all this broke. You can just imagine how Ilana was labeled. In fact, I've been a friend of the whole Kloss family for years, and Ilana's mother always stays at our apartment when she visits New York. But it doesn't matter. I know there will be mean whispers from now on, whoever I happen to be with. When a friend told me what some people were gossiping about me and a woman friend, I finally just blew my top and I screamed out, "Does this mean I can never again have a friend who's female?"

Well, does it?

But there have been some nice things to come out of all this. I think I know better now who really cares about me, who I can count on. I was very touched by the way many friends proved they really were friends.

And my brother; poor Randy, it was hard for him. The Giants were on the road when the news came out, so he was very visible. Nobody can be more crude and insensitive, I suppose, than a team of young men (unless possibly it would be a team of young women), and Randy was sitting on the team bus after the game that night, trying to lie low and be as inconspicuous as possible. Suddenly Darrell Evans came by, and he saw Randy, and he stopped and clapped Randy on the shoulder and said, "Tough day, huh, Moffitt?" and Randy nodded, and then Evans patted him again and said, "Don't worry," and all of a sudden all the other guys were piping up and telling Randy they were behind him, they were behind me.

And then the letters. So many people wrote me, and almost all in support, to tell me they were for me or they loved me. It was the very young or the very old who seemed to write the most letters, but they came from everywhere, from all sorts of people. Then, after a while, the general content of the letters began to change, and the people were not only writing me that they cared but they were going on to tell me something about themselves—and usually something about their sexuality. I mean, they were confessing. After Larry and I did the television interview with Barbara Walters, I received a lovely three-page letter from one of the crew, telling me all about his private life, all about himself. Most often the mail had nothing to do with homosexuality, either. People just wanted me to know something private about themselves, as the world now knew something private about me.

Isn't it ironic? For so long, so many people thought of me as a tough bitch, and suddenly, when I was exposed, I guess I stopped being a threat any longer. More than that; I had been betrayed. Had anyone ever been so cruel to a friend as Marilyn was to me? I was very vulnerable, and so people felt impelled to reach out and join with me. Not only that; but in many cases they thought somehow that I might be able to help them, that my adversity had made me wiser. And maybe it did.

Another thing about this response I've noticed is that it hasn't just been women who have been approaching me. In fact, this was starting to be more of the case even before all of the personal publicity. Little boys would come up to me, ask me questions about tennis, tell me they were a fan of mine. Why, some of them would even say I was their favorite. Maybe after all these years what I had been trying to say was finally getting through. More and more I could see that I was being perceived as an athlete first, and then as an athlete who happens to be a woman.

Of course, my days as a full-time athlete were numbered even before news of the affair came out. Tennis is the kind of game that if I stay in shape I can always pop back in now and then, especially in doubles. I mean, after all, Stolle and Newcombe got to the semifinals of the 1981 U.S. Open. It's certainly possible, too, that some kind of over-thirty-five or over-forty-five women's tour will start up, as with the men. Maybe I'll have to do something about that.

But I was prepared to take myself out as a full-time touring player even before Marilyn filed her suit. Like almost every athlete, I know I'll have trouble making that adjustment in my life. But yes, while I always dreaded the fact that someday I would have to give it up, I also think I prepared myself better for it than most players. As I said, if you've been number one and then you can't be number one anymore, you're already finished. In a way, I've known that I was just a shell of a player for years. Besides, with all my injuries, all my operations, all my time in hospitals, I've had the opportunity to assess myself, to understand how physically vulnerable any athlete is.

After all, I was so conscious of this sort of change of life that I took myself out of the game prematurely in 1975. Looking back, I know that was a mistake. Larry never could understand my rationale for that move, and he was right. I learned very quickly that I had retired too soon, and the funny thing is that I've always thought I could have won Wimbledon again in 1976. I was there to play doubles, and I was in great shape, and it was unusually hot; I never felt better in London. And, of course, I was hitting with everybody because all the players wanted to use me as a trial horse.

But then, the single thing I regret about my career is that I never planned it very well—not in a long-term, overall way. I never sat down and said, I want to do this, I want to aim for that, I'll set this goal. I'm sure I could have won more than twenty Wimbledon titles if I'd plotted things better. I'm sure I could have won a lot more big titles all over. But I never designed anything. I just sort of drifted into tennis, and I kept on drifting along, especially when all the injuries began to chop me up. All I ever wanted to be was the best, but I never defined that in any practical way.

Yes, but maybe if I had worked it all out when I was young, maybe if I had set up all these strictly tennis goals, then maybe I wouldn't have had the time to be Jackie Robinson. I think, when I'm old and gray and I look back, it will feel better that I won a lot of titles, but that I also was Jackie Robinson. And somebody like Chris or Margaret, when they're old and gray and they look back, it will only be the titles they see. The best part of all is creating. That's better than just winning something that's already there.

That's one reason why I'm especially excited about being the commissioner of Team Tennis. Now I'll admit it: I got the job by sleeping with the boss. Larry brought Team Tennis back to life in 1980, and I'm sure it will work in the new way he has designed it. I'm especially confident because I know that the old World Team Tennis never should have folded. The owners tanked it—acting like a bunch of babies, just like the players. At the time, 1978, when the league was folded, WTT was drawing 25 percent of the tennis crowds in the world, and average attendance had gone from seventeen hundred to fifty-seven hundred per match, while the league's losses were down from ten million to one million. Of all my disappointments, that was my biggest one, when WTT gave up—because it didn't have to. And you see, I don't believe in

Team Tennis merely as a business enterprise. I want to see it established at all age levels. The trouble now is that boys and girls don't play together as youngsters. They don't share the same experiences, as they would with Team Tennis.

Having that job has reinvigorated me. It made me look up and out, away from myself. I was so tired there for a while, so sad, so worn out. Sometimes I thought I just should go away and hide somewhere, think, read books, finally learn to play the piano, as my mother wanted so much. I'm still thinking, too, that maybe now at last is the time for us to have that baby—or, anyway, to adopt one. Maybe. And now that I'm through with this book, my own story, I want to write one about the history of women's tennis. I want to sit down one day and talk to Suzanne Lenglen—the best I can, anyway.

As miserable as I was, I never packed it in. Dennis Wasser, our lawyer, couldn't believe it when he saw Larry and me together right after my press conference. I mean, this was about the bottom of my life. And Larry kissed me, and he said, "Hey, Billie Jean, if you could have one wish now, what would it be?"

And just like that, I kissed Larry back and I said, "Oh, beautiful, long, skinny legs."

That just blew Dennis's mind. He said then he knew for sure I'd be okay.

So I'm not going to just wash away. I promise you that. I'm going to keep on trying. You know, I've never really cared what anybody did so long as they tried at it. I just plain like people who try. It doesn't matter what, so long as they get out there and work their bahoolas off.